Father Francis MacNutt's new book is
a moving and powerful testimony to
the healing action of the spirit.

THE POWER TO HEAL

"A great addition to the library on healing! It not
only arouses faith but it clarifies many points that
have been a mystery and in some cases a barrier to
those who pray for healing."

—Agnes Sanford
Author of *Healing Gifts of the Spirit*

"The most helpful book on healing that I have read.
Father MacNutt deals directly with the difficult
issues in the area of physical healing."

—Michael Scanlan
Author of *Inner Healing*

"An invaluable resource to those who minister in
faith to the sick. It should be required reading for
anyone presently engaged in a sacramental ministry
of healing."

—Donald Gelpi, S.J.
Author of *Pentecostalism—A Theological Viewpoint*

"Father MacNutt has a great gift for bringing the
reality of God's healing Presence into our human
suffering."

—Barbara Shlemon
Author of *Healing Prayer*

THE POWER TO HEAL

Francis MacNutt, o.p.

This low-priced Bantam Book has been completely reset in a type face designed for easy reading, and was printed from new plates. It contains the complete text of the original hard-cover edition. NOT ONE WORD HAS BEEN OMITTED.

THE POWER TO HEAL
For information address: Ave Maria Press,
Notre Dame, Ind. 46556.

*This low-priced Bantam Book
has been completely reset in a type face
designed for easy reading, and was printed
from new plates. It contains the complete
text of the original hard-cover edition.*
NOT ONE WORD HAS BEEN OMITTED

THE POWER TO HEAL

A Bantam Book published by arrangement with
Ave Maria Press

PRINTING HISTORY
Ave Maria Press edition published July 1977
2nd printing... October 1977
3rd printing... June 1978

Bantam edition/May 1979

English translation of excerpts from the Rite of Anointing and Pastoral Care of
the Sick © *1973, and* The Sacramentary © *1974, by permission of International
Committee on English in the Liturgy, Inc*

Back cover photograph by Quinta Scott

*Bantam Books are published by Bantam Books, Inc Its trademark, consisting of
the words "Bantam Books" and the portrayal of a bantam, is Registered in U S.
Patent and Trademark Office and in other countries. Marca Registrada. Bantam
Books, Inc , 666 Fifth Avenue, New York, New York 10019*

PRINTED IN THE UNITED STATES OF AMERICA

Contents

Part Four: Special Questions

Preface

In the three years since I wrote *Healing* I have had many unusual experiences in praying for healing—some of them apparent failures—and I have participated in many discussions with friends involved in the healing ministry. Through all this I have come to both deeper understanding and a few new insights that I haven't found in other books on the subject. So I am very anxious to share them with a larger public than is able to attend our workshops. What we have discovered, for instance, about the importance of the time element in healing is, I think, a real breakthrough in this ministry.

It's not as if we've had to revise any of the basic teaching we learned earlier; it's more like we've deepened our understanding of what the Lord had taught us over the years.

Taught *us*, I say, because I have been genuinely blessed in being able to work with a team most of the time, traveling all over the United States as well as to Europe, Latin America, Africa, the Orient and Australia. These team members have included Mrs. Barbara Shlemon, Father Michael Scanlan, T.O.R., Sister Jeanne Hill, O.P., Father Paul Schaaf, C.Pp.S., Rev. Tommy Tyson, Mrs. Ruth Carter Stapleton, Dr. Conrad Baars, Fathers

Matt and Denny Linn, S.J., and many others, who have helped put on healing workshops and then reflected with me on what we found happening as we prayed with the sick.

At Merton House, my home in St. Louis, Sister Mary Margaret, V.H.M., Sister Miriam Young, O.P., Dr. Daryl Anderson and others have helped me these past few years, sharing what they have learned about long-term patient concern in the day-to-day ministry of inner healing.

In all we do we have tried to build on the foundation we first received from Mrs. Agnes Sanford and other pioneers in the healing ministry.

One of the beautiful things I have experienced in this ministry of healing is that all of us who have worked together over the years have been gifted with a real love for one another, as well as with a remarkable unity of outlook—almost as if we had all been learning the same things at the same time. This sharing with one another, over refreshments, after a long session of praying, has been a great gift!

The subject of this book will be limited to prayer for healing in general and to *physical healing* in particular. Sometime later I hope to write a book about inner healing, and after that, another on prayer for deliverance. The present book will be necessarily limited in scope; it presupposes that you have read a book (such as *Healing*) that is more orderly in its development. The chapters here will be more like a sharing of various discoveries and insights. It won't be comprehensive—like a body of teaching—nor will it touch upon such important subjects as healing in community. But, if you are in the healing ministry, I think some of these insights will prove as exciting and helpful to you as they have been for us.

I want to thank my friends in Clearwater, Florida, who have provided a place of escape in which I was able to write undisturbed, as well as other friends such as Sister Aimee Marie Spahn, O.S.F. (Dubuque, Iowa), Mrs. Barb Enlow, and Mrs. Betty Holmes, who have offered their time and typing skill.

Most of all I want to thank God for wonderful friends who have been his greatest healing gift to me.

Francis S. MacNutt, O.P.

Introduction
Healing Through Prayer—
A Rediscovery

In the past 10 years, my understanding of the power of Jesus Christ to transform people's lives has been gradually, but radically, changed. Not that I ever doubted that he came to transform our lives, but I thought he did it mainly through his teachings. He was the prophet and teacher who pointed the way for us to follow. And not only did he teach and point the way, but he was also our model: the Way, the Truth and the Life.

All this is true, of course. But I didn't fully realize that we need his *power* to transform us—that we can't just teach and preach, and then expect people to be changed.

THE DEPTH OF OUR WOUND

In my early adult years, during high school and college, I came to the recognition of a degree of weakness, of powerlessness in people that I had never fully realized was there. During two years in the Army in World War II, I had seen contrasts of human goodness and sin that I had never known in a protected childhood and a world of private schools and colleges. The Army brought me into contact with a world of people whom, by and large, I could not trust; I didn't need to believe in sin—I could really see that our world was somehow under its sway. I was naively bewildered by the mystery of sin. Why were people so cruel and hard?

Then, after several more protected years in the seminary, I met evil again after ordination. Only now, instead of meeting people who were evil or seemed willingly caught up in evil, I met *good* people who came to me asking for help. They came to confession or asked for spiritual direction during a retreat; they were good people who somehow were trapped in one (or more) areas of life that seemed evil. And they couldn't free themselves by willpower. Spiritual and psychological lack of freedom was tormenting them. The depressed person who contemplated suicide couldn't be free by desiring to be free; the married homosexual suffering from his sexual struggles could not free himself to love his wife; there were those, including myself, suffering from anxiety—what was the answer, when Christ told us we should not be anxious? Then there were the people (including a priest who lived in the same house with me) suffering from such sickness as alcoholism. All these people who came to me for help were already going to confession and presumably were repentant.

In the course of several years, I came to realize that many—perhaps most—of the suffering people who came to me for spiritual direction were burdened by real evil that did not give way to repentance or willpower. Their plaint echoed Paul's: "... I have been sold as a slave to sin. I cannot understand my own behavior. I fail to carry out the things I want to do, and I find myself doing the very things I hate" (Rm 7:14-15). People were coming to me and looking for help after admitting things that brought them to tears—sins they did not really want to commit, but which they were somehow driven to. A man, for instance, might feel driven by loneliness to get into his car and head for a nearby city, cruising until he found another man in a park or bar. He would feel terrible remorse and shame, but somehow he couldn't stop such encounters for more than a few days at a time. At the end of a week, it would happen all over again. He would feel wrong about his confessions because he was always falling and confessing the same thing. What could I say that would help him?

Or what could I say to a nun who felt so miserable about life that she felt like committing suicide? I could discourage the suicide, but did my words really affect the depression?

A PSYCHOLOGICAL SOLUTION

It was about that time that.I—and many priests like me—began to read books on counseling and psychology. We began to realize that much personal behavior seemed to be determined by past experiences for which the individual was not responsible. It became increasingly difficult to separate spiritual problems from psychological ones. Some articles (and much private conversation) by moral theologians suggested that masturbation was not always a sin—certainly not a serious sin—but simply part of the process of growing up. We were told that many things we had been labeling as sins, such as alcoholism, were more like sicknesses. We could not just tell the person to repent and shape up; he needed help—a doctor, a guest house.

If these various problems that tormented people were not voluntary, but were simply part of a process of growing up, then the best thing a preacher or counselor could do was to help the person to understand this behavior as part of a process, rather than to label it as sin or evil. When a person cannot change his behavior, labeling his actions as sin simply increases his anxiety by making him feel guilty and hated by God for behavior that he cannot change. Eventually, the behavior might change, but not at this moment, so it seemed healthier for the priest-counselor to accept these persons (whom we once would have labeled sinners) as they were, rather than condemning them and thus leading them to condemn themselves, worsening their condition.

On the face of it, that accepting attitude seemed to be a more loving attitude than our previous one. For a time, it seemed that the best way to help people suffering from what had appeared to be incurable spiritual problems was to send them to the psychiatrist.

But many were not helped by the psychiatrists, either. What was the answer? The problem involved more than healing *this person;* it involved how we understood life in general in the light of redemption, when so much human sickness seemed to be more destructive than redemptive. How could I speak of the love of Jesus Christ to a woman paralyzed by deep mental depression? If I tried to encourage her by saying that God loved her, she would answer: "Maybe God loves you, but he surely doesn't love me. Just look at me. I even hate myself. If he loved me, he wouldn't leave me in this state."

As you can see, I was simply trying to make sense out of the kind of mess that causes so many Christians to lose faith. It was the same situation we all confront at times in our lives, and would like to forget: the age-old problem of evil. None of the answers I had been preaching up to that point in my life was satisfying when it came face to face with reality. To call all these human problems sin, as though the sufferers could change their lives through repentance, was clearly a hard line that sometimes worked and sometimes didn't. Some people could change; some couldn't. Some of it was personal sin, but some of it was mixed with a lack of inner freedom so that the person simply couldn't change without help.

But were psychology and the power of human love enough to change deep-rooted problems? Sometimes counseling helped, but many times it simply wasn't enough. Especially it often wasn't enough to help those hurting the most. Articles began to appear in *Psychology Today*, questioning whether psychiatry was really worth all that money when just about as many patients (approximately one-third) got better who had no treatment as those who had undergone extensive psychoanalysis. So, what was the answer? Are there a certain number of people who are hopeless, as it were, and should just learn to accept their condition and endure life as a test, but without much happiness? If that kind of cynical solution seemed realistic, it also eviscerated the Gospel and made it relatively meaningless when it talked about Good News and salvation. What did it mean, anyway, to say that Jesus is the one who saves, who redeems mankind? Maybe I could lift all that up to some abstract, sermonic level, but what does it mean when you are trying to help a weeping friend who is contemplating suicide?

POWER TO HEAL

I share all this personal searching because, in some way, we all go through it, trying to make some sense out of the mystery of human suffering. It was in this questing frame of mind that I first heard, in 1966, of someone who had a strong belief that Jesus Christ would heal people if we asked   and this person had many successful healings to back up that theory. Actually, it is a very simple concept which corresponds to a literal interpretation of the Gospel passages that speak about Jesus healing the people who came crowding around him. It is the Gospel of Mark, probably the earliest written, that makes special note of the crowds of people coming for healing, often making it impossible for Jesus and the disciples to eat. Sometimes Jesus had to cross the lake or even go to gentile territory just to escape the multitudes who gave him no rest in their search for healing. The number of these references in the Gospel is impressive; it seemed to me that it was easier to understand these crowds and healing scenes as having really happened than to reinterpret them symbolically.

So, when I heard that people were praying directly for healing, laying hands on the sick and all that, it seemed important to check it out. The people I heard and later met like Agnes Sanford impressed me as being intelligent, sincere and filled with a hopeful faith that I envied. Not only did they have hope, but a wealth of experience, in seeing healing happen. What I regarded as extraordinary was simply their shoptalk. Eventually I, in turn, decided to take the risk of faith and began to pray in a *personal* way for the sick—I stopped just saying *general* prayers at a distance. It was then that my understanding began to change and I saw that certain elements in Catholic tradition had more substance than I thought.

Original sin is, I now find, a very real thing—not merely an abstraction. It is a real evil in human beings, but at the same time it is not personal sin, as though the person desires to be afflicted. We are all wounded: our wills don't always have the power to change, our minds are confused, our emotions can enslave us, and we are strangely moved by unreasoning impulses. Admitting that man is basically good and created by God, there still is an evil within us that is also somehow beyond us. There is also evil outside us and, as St. Paul says, our struggles are not just against flesh and blood but against principalities and powers. (At times now I find that I have to command evil spirits to leave people in order for them to be set free.)

All this, I know, sounds primitive to some theologians writing today, who are now claiming that prayer of petition dominates the minds of prescientific cultures, and that the predominance of science in the Western mentality since the Copernican revolution has gradually relegated prayer as petition to the status of superstition. Such a view asserts that it is a negative spirituality which emphasizes man's limitation, and fails to respect the unlimited capacity of humanity to know and affect the universe.

What I see is something quite different; I am a Christian humanist, who does not overly stress the negative aspects of life, but I see the Gospel speaking of our *dependence* upon God and our need—our desperate need of a savior. Like St. Paul, I find that it is impossible to prevent myself from doing the very thing I hate without the saving power of Christ.

And I have seen too many people sit before me, pouring out their life history, and then finding them hopeless to pull themselves out, humanly speaking. There is a limit to the power of human beings to achieve their own perfection.

Over and over again I have seen that there is a power, the saving, healing power of Jesus Christ, which can change and transform lives in ways that I never would have dreamed of in my previous pastoral experience.

Not only that, but I find doctors and counselors quite willing now to admit the limits of their science. (Already 24 doctors are registered to make a workshop on prayer for healing that is to be held two months from the time I write this.) Some doctors and scientists, of course, hold to the view quoted above about the sufficiency of science and human nature, but on the whole I find them quite open to investigate the evidence relating to prayer for healing (more open, at times, than theologians, priests and ministers). In one instance, a doctor who prayed for his patients was reported to the hospital administration by the chaplain for unprofessional conduct. (The doctor was exonerated, and it was pointed out that he brought more patients to the hospital than any other physician.)

The simplest way to interpret the gospel, and to understand the love of God is to affirm that if God has the power to help someone suffering from a sickness that is destructive of human personality, he *would do* something, and whatever he would do is clearly far more than something I might do. This is what the Gospel says in so many ways: "If you, then, who are evil, know how to give your children what is good, how much more will your Father in heaven give good things to those who ask him!" (Mt 7:11).

To speak of this power of Jesus to heal the sick is my desire in this book. If you are not convinced, I invite you to pray for the sick, or accompany those who do, and find out for yourself. For me, three things have combined to convince me:

1. *The Human Situation Cries Out for an Answer*

As I mentioned earlier, we are in a dismal pastoral situation where we find people who are really trying to live good lives, who have tried to change and yet are still suffering from sickness—especially spiritual and emotional sickness—that is wearing them down and does not appear to be redemptive. Often they are tempted to doubt the love and mercy of God. If there is not power to heal beyond the human methods they have already tried, what kind of answer can we give to them when they ask about God's will? Like Ivan in *Brothers Karamazov*, some Christians who have searched deeply into human suffering have ended up as atheists because they see Christianity as preaching *acceptance* of evil as God's will. They cannot put that together with God's love. Sometimes a greater good can come out of a sickness and sickness can be accepted as a necessary evil; but sickness is in itself evil and we need to speak more about real healing power and God's desire to bring wholeness to us, either in this life or the next. Often we need his transforming power to heal in *this* life.

Someone has said that a true Christian cannot stand by, looking at suffering humanity, with folded arms. But the way I preached about sickness was as if God did precisely that: watched suffering humanity with arms folded, all the while saying, "It will do you good."[1]

The passionate questioning of the sick people and their families is better answered by saying, as a general rule, that "an enemy has done this" and "God is on your side," and, "if we pray he will bring some kind of help and healing to you."

2. *The Gospel Addresses That Human Situation*

This basic human dilemma of sickness is directly addressed by the Gospel. The simplest (and traditional) understanding of the Christian message is that:

a) Mankind is suffering from a primordial sinful

---

[1] This calls to mind a letter I recently received which reads, in part: "Sadly, our religious strength has not come from Catholic priests. They give communion, mumble a blessing, and are gone in seconds. My husband's fellowship has come from Protestants. We thank the Lord that when we needed prayer, he sent someone to us who could strengthen us."

situation (original sin) from which it is powerless to extricate itself. The Old Testament is a record of God calling and rescuing his chosen people and of their failing to live up to that call.

b) Then Jesus came to free us, to save, to heal us from the effects of that sin. That sin is not only personal ("Your sins are forgiven"—Lk 7:48) but is part of the situation into which we are born ("And this woman, a daughter of Abraham whom Satan has bound these 18 years—was it not right to untie her bonds on the sabbath day?" [Lk 13:16]). In *Acts* Peter gives a brief summation of the public ministry of Jesus: "Because God was with him, Jesus went about doing good and curing all who had fallen into the power of the devil" (Acts 10:38). Jesus freed people not only from sin but also from bodily sickness, which is seen, at least *indirectly*, as the effect of sin (for the most part, not personal sin, but the fallen human condition).

c) The Gospel speaks of this power to free and to heal being passed on to the Church: "He called the 12 together and gave them power and authority over all devils and to cure diseases, and he sent them out to proclaim the kingdom of God and to heal" (Lk 9:1-2). It seems clear from this and many other passages that authority and power are passed on to the Church. Not that we have ever doubted this in doctrine or theory, but there has been a practical doubt, a lack of faith, when we come to apply it in our pastoral practice.

For example, if a young drug addict comes to me for help, suffering from that sickness which is clearly not redemptive—do I believe that he will be freed from this enslaving habit if I ask Christ to free him?

3. *My Experience*

If the previous considerations about our understanding of God's compassion and the meaning of redemption as revealed in scripture were not enough to persuade me that there should be a power in Jesus Christ to heal, my own recent experience would be more than enough to convince me. For most of us, experience is what really convinces; the people who remain skeptical about healing are, I find, people talking from outside, as it were—who have not seen the kind of things that I have been privileged to see. After the 72 came back rejoicing at the healings and exorcisms they had performed, Jesus (after telling them to rejoice, rather, that their names were written in heaven) was filled with joy because the Father had revealed these things to mere children, even though many prophets and kings had wanted to see what the 72 were now seeing. What they had just seen was the power to heal and to tread underfoot the whole power of the enemy (Lk 10:17-24).

In the past eight years it has been a joy for me to see many people freed, healed, or strengthened by the power of Jesus Christ released through prayer. Many of the things I have seen are so wonderful as to sound incredible to those who have not themselves experienced them. These saving actions of God include spiritual healings (such as being freed instantly from long-standing alcoholism), emotional healings (such as from schizophrenia and deep mental depression), and physical healings (such as growths disappearing in a matter of minutes). For some these healings are immediate; for some they are gradual and take months, and for still others nothing at all seems to happen. But I would estimate that about 75 percent of the people we pray for, for physical or emotional ailments, are either healed completely or experience a noticeable improvement. Almost everyone regards the prayer as a real blessing and experiences the presence of Christ in a very direct way.

I would encourage any of you who question all this—and we usually do question the authenticity of healing through prayer when we first hear about it to check it out for yourself. Healing is caused by far more than the power of suggestion or even what can be achieved through the love of a compassionate person.

Let me just share part of a letter dated May 7, 1976, the kind of letter that often comes to me:

I am writing to tell you of a miracle which has happened. I hope you might remember me: I am the one who was a drug addict. You advised me to get in touch with ——and I did this last October. The struggles I had were unbelievable. I found a retired Anglican priest here...who discerns carefully between mental problems which are psychological and those which are spiritual. I was delivered from the demons of lust and drugs only two months ago and since then my life in the Christian therapy group I'm in has bloomed so much that I'm soon to leave it with everyone's consent. I am having NO trouble with lust or drugs; I am at peace totally in a relationship with Jesus Christ and I praise God for it daily in a gentle, quiet way. Father, I am at peace for the first time in 31 years! . . .

Seeing hundreds of people like this man—the kind of case I would have written off 10 years ago as nearly hopeless and a waste of my time—completely healed, or at least helped, by the power of prayer has helped me, too, see the love of God for his people in a deeper way than ever before. A whole new world has opened up for me.

I trust that this wonderful power to heal is going to be rediscovered by the Church and by the medical profession and that this will lead us into an era we would not have dreamed of just a few short years ago.

PART ONE

New Insights Into Healing

a very faulty notion of what they are doing, which in turn
will spiritually and psychologically harm those they pray

"Then putting spittle on his eyes and
laying his hands on him, he asked, 'Can
you see anything?' The man, who was
beginning to see, replied, 'I can see
people; they look like trees to me, but
they are walking about.' Then he laid his
hands on the man's eyes again and he
saw clearly." (Mark 8:23-25)

1. The More and the Less

The most important thing I have learned in the past few years about praying for healing is that *usually* people are not completely healed by prayer, but they are *improved*.

Looking at that statement now, it seems fairly obvious. Most things in life are that way. Healing through medicine is that way. We go to a doctor and come away happy as long as healing has begun and improvement has been shown. We are overjoyed if the doctor holds out hope that in a week or a month the body will be completely restored to wholeness.

But in some preaching and writing on healing there is a kind of absoluteness that makes it imperative that all healing through prayer be immediate. "Can you claim your healing now" puts many sick people in a bind; they want to show faith in God by saying "yes," but they want to be honest, too, and say, "But I still can't walk so I'm not sure." The observable healings that take place at large healing services are, of their nature, immediate—or else, they take place in a relatively short time span (for instance, a tumor may take 10 minutes to disappear). Those Christians who attend large healing services are led to think in terms of "Am I healed right now or not?"

Even though I have always tried to keep a balance in my teaching and ministry, I realize now that I, too, had taken on something of that all-or-nothing, black-or-white mentality. For instance, I would ask after a healing service, "How many of you, in all honesty, feel that the Lord has healed you?" And then, because I wanted to be honest and get some idea of what was happening, I would ask, "And how many of you don't feel any change has taken place?" Most evangelists never ask that question, so

I felt I was moving courageously in the direction of honesty. After some meetings almost 80 percent would raise their hands to indicate that they had experienced healing; at other meetings only about 20 percent would raise their hands. I knew that this was only a subjective recording of impressions, and that such a show of hands was in no way a scientific proof that would impress professional people, such as doctors. But it was a help, an indication of how powerfully God was working in a particular group, and I kept learning more and more from such questionong as to how God worked and which conditions in a healing service seemed to help.

But I always noticed a number of people raising their hands tentatively—not sure in which group they belonged.

It was only later that I learned that I really needed to ask another question: "How many of you are not completely well, but definitely feel improved through the prayer?" Since learning to ask these three questions, instead of just two, I have found, as a general rule, that about 25 percent of the people indicate that they are completely healed, 50 percent are improved, and for about 25 percent nothing much seems to happen.[1]

This indicates that for many people—probably for most people—a single prayer for healing is not sufficient. What they need is the continued prayer of another person or a group.

This parallels the encouraging example of Jesus himself who had to pray twice with a blind man (Mk 8:22-26). The first time Jesus prayed, the man was greatly improved—he "was beginning to see." But he wasn't completely cured; the people he saw looked as if they were trees walking around. So even Jesus had to lay his hands on the man's eyes once again; then the man saw clearly.

So, if even Jesus had to pray for a person twice, we can

---

[1] This, of course, is only a very rough approximation, based only on some healing services in which I have taken part. The only thing I want to point out is that it seems that the majority of people I pray with are not completely healed at the first prayer, nor are they untouched by God's healing power; but they are improved.

certainly expect to have to pray three times or more for the chronic sufferers who come to us for help. This much has become abundantly clear: prayer for healing is *often a process. It requires time.*

The cruelest thing a minister of healing can do is to tell a person whose ailment has improved through his prayer, "Now, you must believe that you have been healed. To pray again would be for you to lack faith in God."

Over and over again I have had to pick up the pieces—to reassure sick people who definitely felt something happen when they were prayed for, but who continued to experience the symptoms of their sickness and began to despair, because they felt they lacked faith. In so many cases, the problem is not with the sick people but with the ministers of healing who lack wisdom. Yet they speak in tones of such authority that the timid believe that the ministers speak with the authority of God.

Looking back now, I remember some patients we prayed for who had cancer. And some of them were healed. I remember in particular one man who had lung cancer that completely disappeared (as was verified by X-rays). Then, a year later, cancer reappeared in the intestinal area. To me the simplest explanation would be that most of the cancer was cured; but a small number of cancerous cells remained which later began to grow again and spread to another part of the body. If we had not been so anxious to proclaim a healing, we would have continued to pray with him at other times afterwards, to burn out, through God's healing power, those last remnants of cancer that later grew and spread in another part of his body.

I learned something along this line just last summer. We were praying for a woman with a severe back problem. A doctor was present and tested the various areas of the back before we prayed. Then we prayed until all the pain seemed to leave and the woman was able to move about freely without pain. So far as I could tell, she was cured, and our prayer was ended. But the doctor then touched various areas in her back to see what had happened; in one area he was still able to make her wince.

He said, "This is amazing; I've never seen anything like this occur so fast. She's about 95 percent improved; but here's still an area that's not completely right." So we prayed again until even that was gone. The point, of course, is that I—as a layman in medical matters—was not aware that she was still not fully healed and needed more prayer.

It is not surprising, then, that when we are dealing with something like cancer, which is much harder to detect than a misaligned spine, it is also more difficult to declare it completely healed. Unless we receive a revelation from God to the effect that it has been healed, we would be rash to tell people that they should claim a total healing, just because they have experienced some relief through our prayer. What I have learned to do, therefore, is to ask people to come back for further prayer as a precaution and as a blessing when the sickness is as serious as cancer—even after it seems to be gone—until the doctors are able to verify that the person is cured.

PRACTICAL CONCLUSIONS

Two Cases

The following is typical of the kind of improvement that we often see take place without total healing: (This letter was written a year after praying for her):

> I was born crippled and cross-eyed. After you prayed for me my eyes became straighter, my back became straight, my left foot straighter, my left leg lengthened the same as the right. I have no more limp. My legs are improving gradually. My heels used to stick out much more, my knees used to go forward much more; they're now almost straight. I lie flat on my back and try to make my toes meet and they miss by about four inches   which is a great improvement.

A further remarkable story of improvement comes from a woman who has been in a wheelchair for 20 years because of polio.

When you and Sister Jeanne prayed with me last year my leg lengthened, but nothing else seemed to materialize.

My husband took me to the May, 1975, Rome Conference. Monday at Mass in St. Peter's Basilica a stranger came up to me (I was just behind the music ministry group) and said that the Lord was standing in the dome with his hands stretched over me and would heal me. I thought, "Oh heavens, another one of those people!" I thanked her and turned back to trying to see (you can't see much from a wheelchair). A little later she returned and told me to claim the healing power of the Eucharist when I received communion. A girl in the music group shared a portion of her host with me. Then I was enveloped in warmth, and wave after wave of something like electricity nearly knocked me out of my chair. My husband thought I was ill or something, but after the initial surprise I realized what was happening. The woman reappeared and told me to claim the healing and not to doubt, because it would not be all at once. Then she disappeared and I have not seen her since. But God continues to work with me, and, day by day, I find myself stronger and able to do things I haven't done in 20 years! My S-curvature is gone, my shoulders are even and my body is in alignment. The left side of my face no longer sags. (It felt like all my bones were being rearranged, and I believe they were.) I can turn to both left and right in my chair to look behind me! I can eat without using the elbow for leverage! I can lift my left leg and hip off the chair! I can cross both legs. I can hold my left arm halfway up to praise the Lord. I can embrace my husband with that arm for the first time in 20 years. The hip muscles are getting stronger, as is the right leg, making lifting much easier. The right arm hasn't begun to move yet, but it will.

In the repeated prayer sessions, we don't need to begin all over again, as it were, as though we had never prayed before; we can *continue* the prayer begun at an earlier time, just asking that the life and healing power of Jesus enter into every cell of the person's body.

Or, in our reiterated prayers, we can simply pray in tongues, asking the Spirit to pray through us for whatever is best at this time for this person. ("The Spirit, too, comes to help us in our weakness. For when we cannot choose words in order to pray properly, the Spirit himself expresses our plea in a way that could never be put into words..." Rm 8:26.)

When people say that they have "lost their healing," one of the possible explanations is simply this: they thought the healing was complete; but something of the ailment was still left, which later grew back.

For all these reasons, I have found my ability to help the sick has greatly increased by recognizing that—

1) There is a *time element* in most healing. Even in healings that seem instant there is at least a period of minutes in which the change takes place.

2) There is also an element of *more or less power*, more or less authority in me, since I am not God, but only share in his life, so that the effect of my prayer on the sickness may not completely dispel the sickness and bring in the wholeness of life. (I am a "wounded healer.")

3) In consequence, many of the people I pray with are not completely healed but are *improved*.

These understandings result in the following changes in my ministry of healing:

1) I must get out of the habit of thinking of all people in categorical terms as healed by prayer or not healed by prayer. I should rejoice if many—or even some—of the people I pray for experience some of God's healing power and are improved in health.

2) I want to grow closer in union with Jesus Christ, so that more of his life, his wisdom, his authority and his healing power will work through me to heal others. But this, too, is a process and takes time. While not being complacent, I shall be patient, knowing that growth is an organic process.

3) I will learn to be patient with myself and the sick, knowing that more time is often what we need to complete the healing.

Putting this all down on paper makes it seem so simple. The amazing thing is that it takes so long for some people with a powerful ministry of healing to learn it. Perhaps the more powerful and dramatic your ministry is, the harder it will be for you to see not only the YES and the NO, the healed and the sick, but THE MORE AND THE LESS, the slightly improved illness, and the long-process growth.

2. Healing Through Touch

When I first began to learn about praying for healing I wanted to learn how to say the prayer of faith, how to frame the words. I knew that the laying on of hands was important, but I saw it as subsidiary to the prayer I said. But now I have come to realize that touch can be a prayer that has a power all its own.

It's clear that sometimes Jesus healed only through words or desire, as when he told the Canaanite woman who asked that her daughter be healed at a distance, "Woman, you have great faith. Let your wish be granted." At that moment her daughter was well again (Mt 16:28).

But for others he said not a word; his touch alone healed. The woman with the flow of blood sneaked through the crowd and was healed when she touched the hem of his garment (Mk 5:28). He apparently didn't even know about her presence until he became "aware that power had gone out from him" (Mk 5:30). Again, we read:

> When the local people recognized him they spread the news through the whole neighborhood and took all who were sick to him, begging him just to let them touch the fringe of his cloak. And all those who touched it were completely cured (Mt. 14:35-36).

So the prayer, or perhaps we should say the power, for healing does not depend always on a spoken prayer. The touch of Jesus in itself brings healing.[1]

---

[1] Ordinarily, from the Gospel accounts, it seems that Jesus both touched the person and commanded the sickness to leave; the word and the touch were both present.

Now, is there any significance in all this for those of us in a healing ministry?

I think there is. I didn't see it very well in the beginning, but now I am beginning to realize why Jesus heals through touch, as well as through spoken prayer.

TIMES WHEN WE CANNOT SPEAK

There are many times, especially when visiting patients in a hospital, when it is inappropriate to disturb patients or nurses by praying out loud (for instance, late at night in an intensive care unit). Just being there, holding the patient's hand—with or without quiet prayer—can be the channel for God's healing power. Our culture is very verbal, and I have to admit that unless I can say a prayer, at least under my breath, I usually don't feel comfortable. But I think that is my weakness. If I had more trust in God, I wouldn't need to feel that I had to say anything.

I know a sister who is a nurse; every morning when she goes to work she asks Jesus to use her hands to heal and comfort, to let them be his hands. Then she simply goes about her work in a loving way. She finds that the patients themselves sense a difference when she gives a back rub, or when she bathes them.

At New York University now there are studies being made—in a nonreligious setting—on the effects of nurses laying hands on patients with the intention of healing. These studies provide evidence to show that, simply in the natural order, the patient's power of recovery improves when the nurses lay on hands. How much more we might expect to happen in an explicitly Christian context.

The way they understand it is that there is a natural power of life in loving people which is communicated in a special way through the power of touch, and that the patient absorbs much of this life, or energy, in such a way that the sick body can build up its own life-building forces.[2]

---

[2] In the *American Journal of Nursing* (May, 1975, pp. 784 ff.) Dolores Krieger describes her experiments teaching nurses at New York University School of Nursing how to lay hands on their patients with the

As Christians we know that we share the very life of God himself (in traditional Catholic terminology: grace) and it makes sense that something of that life-giving power in the physical order can be shared and communicated when we touch a sick person. It seems to me that this current of energy is what so many people feel when we pray for them.

WHEN WE NEED TO PRAY
FOR A LONG TIME

I am also coming to learn that sometimes we don't pray long enough for patients suffering from chronic sickness. If there really is a kind of life-giving power transmitted, a radiation of the life of God, it needs time to work its way through and overcome the sickness and decay already at work killing the healthy tissues of the body.

When we pray for a long time we quickly run out of words to say. Then simply continuing to be there, touching the person   perhaps praying in tongues   seems to be a great help: a powerful prayer in itself.

When I first learned to pray for healing and concentrated on what to say in the prayer, it didn't take very long to say the prayer   a couple of minutes, no more   so there was no need to prolong such a prayer. It's as though, when you say a prayer, you are calling upon

---

intention of healing. She has conducted several studies on patients using the increase in hemoglobin value of the patients' blood as a check on what has happening. In all three tests she conducted she found a significant difference in those patients treated with the laying on of hands. (These studies built upon earlier studies on healing touch conducted by Bernard Grad and Sister Justa Smith.)

Her studies indicate that there may be a natural power in the laying on of hands, provided the nurse has (1) an intent to help heal another and (2) is physically healthy herself. Professor Krieger is "convinced that the practice of therapeutic touch is a natural potential in physically healthy persons who are strongly motivated to help ill people, and that this potential can be actualized" (p. 786).

If the healing touch is a natural potential, Christian prayer uses and elevates this potential to heal, much as the "gift of preaching" builds upon whatever natural speaking talents we may have.

God to do something to help; our part is to ask; any healing that takes place is God's responsibility. Especially when someone telephones long-distance for prayer, and you pray for the sick person over the phone, you are aware that you are really able to do nothing; it's all up to God if anything is going to happen at the other end of the line.

But with the healing that transpires through touch, the healer seems to be more directly involved. Often you will feel something like heat in your hand or in the person you are praying for.[3] At other times you may feel a current of gentle power flow through you. We have long known about such phenomena, and, in *Healing*, I mentioned them in passing. What I am coming to understand now, though, is how some of these sensory phenomena may teach us to pray better. Not that we can ever understand very much about the mystery of God's power. Yet, when we, like Jesus, experience something like a power going out from us, perhaps we can learn something.

The way I understand it (and this is only a surmise) is like this: the Christian shares the life of God himself—that is a certain tenet of Christian belief. The Father, the Son, and the Holy Spirit live within us. Somehow (and here is my conjecture) the energy generated by this life can overflow, can be communicated and flow from one person to another through touching the other person. In all of us there are areas where sickness, sluggishness and death are at work spiritually, emotionally and physically. But when another Christian or a community gathers around to pray, the life, the love and the healing power of Jesus can be transmitted to the sick person.

If there is a great deal of sickness in me, a large cancer for instance, it may *take time* for the radiating power of Jesus to begin to dissolve that cancer.

It's like God's radiation treatment. Just as we know

---

[3] When praying for ailments where there is already inflammation and too much heat in the affected area   such as arthritis   I find that some people experience a wonderful cooling sensation during prayer, rather than the usual heat.

that a single visit of a cancer patient to the hospital to get cobalt radiation treatment is not likely to kill all the cancer cells, so we should not be surprised that it may take more than one session of prayer to cure a chronic illness. I have seen so many sad results from Christians who have prayed once and then have been told to accept their healing as an accomplished fact; sometimes they should "claim their healing," if God reveals to them that they should. But when evangelists do this with everyone they pray for as a matter of principle, I believe that they often do great harm and actually prevent some people from gaining the full healing they would receive if they admitted that they were still sick, and then were free to ask friends to spend more time praying for them. And by time to pray, I mean (a) months or even years of intermittent prayer, or (b) up to eight hours of concentrated prayer at one time.

This is what I call "soaking prayer"—a phrase I first heard from my friend, Reverend Tommy Tyson.

SOAKING PRAYER

"Soaking prayer" conveys the idea of time to let something seep through to the core of something dry that needs to be revived. That's the way it is with the laying on of hands when we feel that God is asking us to take time to irradiate the sickness with his power and love. It is a very gentle prayer.

I first discovered this time factor some years ago in praying with arthritis patients. Suppose we are praying with a person whose hands are crippled with arthritis. I find that such people are occasionally healed, dramatically—usually at large prayer meetings. But, for the most part, when I prayed individually for such people, a little improvement would take place: the fingers would straighten a little, the wrist and fingers would be able to bend a little more; often the pain would be reduced or disappear. In short, there would be a noticeable change, but nothing like a complete healing.

So where do you go from there? Certainly, you can

thank God for the lessening of the pain, and yet you can't say the person was cured. Why such a mixed result?

It was pretty clear that more time for prayer was indicated. I remembered the teachings of Jesus on our need to take time in prayer, to be insistent.

It's significant, for instance, that the famous passage on "Ask, and it will be given to you; search, and you will find; knock, and the door will be opened to you" (Lk 11:9) comes immediately after another passage on asking and knocking, where a man pounds on a friend's door in the middle of the night and gets the natural response, "Don't bother me!" The man keeps shouting and pounding at the door until the man inside gets up. And Jesus observes that if friendship wasn't enough to get him out of bed, the man's "persistence will be enough to make him get up and give his friend all he wants" (Lk 9:8). Many sermons are given on the "Ask, and it will be given to you" section, but the response people are led to seek is often immediate ("Say one prayer and that's enough; if you pray more than that it shows a lack of faith") when clearly Jesus is encouraging us to be as persistent as a man pounding on the door in the middle of the night.

And then there is the story of the widow who keeps hounding the unjust judge to give her a favorable judgment. The judge finally gives in just to have some peace. The teaching that Jesus draws out of it is really startling: "Now will not God see justice done to his chosen who cry to him day and night even when he delays to help them? I promise you, he will see justice done to them, and done speedily. But when the Son of Man comes, will he find any faith on earth?" (Lk 18:7-8). Even the Lord talks about God *delaying* in answering prayer and encourages us to cry out day and night. Then he adds the point that shows his sadness; he seems to see that the time element, the delay, is what occasions our loss of faith in God's power.

In these parables Jesus is telling us to keep on praying; sometimes a single prayer or a single time is not enough. People brought up in the ways of traditional Catholicism are well aware of this—perhaps they are too well aware of it and lack faith that anything will ever really happen—but, on the other hand, people who have learned about prayer from a Pentecostal group may demand immediate answers to prayer and start blaming someone for lack of faith when the sick person isn't instantly and completely cured. If the sick person is cured that way, there are two wonders involved: one in the complete cure; the other in that the cure is immediate and instantaneous.

To get back to the arthritic patient, it just seemed right to spend more time praying to see if anything more would happen. Often enough I found that, if some healing had already started to take place, then further prayer would usually lead to still more healing. As a crude example: if about 10 percent of a healing took place through the first prayer, then, after praying for another 40 minutes, there might be something like a 50 percent improvement.

To me this was a new discovery that I hadn't read anything about. As is usual with a new discovery, it brought a new problem: there just wasn't that kind of time to give to people—especially at large prayer meetings. The more I learned about the time element, the more uncomfortable I felt at seeing people line up for prayer at 10 p.m. after an evening retreat session. Seeing the severity of some of their ailments, I would feel as if I were cheating them by not giving them the time they really needed. I began to realize that some of those people would not be healed tonight, but that they probably could be healed, if only someone had the time to spend soaking them in prayer. In fact, my prayer might make them reluctant to seek out someone else afterwards to pray at length, since I had already prayed; they might feel it a lack of faith on their part to add prayer to prayer. To help them more, I now tell people not to hesitate in seeking someone out to pray at greater length, if they feel improved but not completely healed—that perhaps my prayer will begin their healing and someone else's will finish it.

So I have been teaching people to pray the soaking prayer; for parents to pray for their children; for husbands and wives to pray for each other for all those longtime, deep-down sicknesses that have not responded to briefer prayers. Ailments, such as mental retardation, that are rarely healed in an instant, now seem to be notably improved and occasionally healed, by means of parents soaking the child in prayer over a period of months or years.

THE HOW OF SOAKING PRAYER

Since this kind of prayer takes time we have developed a very simple way of doing it. First comes a prayer, asking God in the ordinary way to heal the person. Then, because there isn't much sense in repetition, we simply continue to lay our hands on the person in such a way that everyone is comfortable. Soaking prayer can be done very much like holding a prayer meeting. After the initial prayer for healing we can alternate periods of song and silence; we can pray in English or we can pray quietly in tongues. As I see it, a kind of life or power continues to pour gently into the affected part all during the time we pray. If a team is praying, then it is easy to change places when someone gets tired. There is no reason why we can't pray for an hour and then take a 10-minute coffee break before coming back to pray again.[4] This continuing prayer can go on as long as we judge is right. Sometimes if we have half a dozen people to pray for, we may linger with one or two for about 10 minutes each. At other times, when we have an appointment with just one person we can pray for anywhere from 10 minutes to a period of hours,

---

[4] Some people still tend to see their lives as separated into distinct parts: holy and secular. They have a hard time feeling right about combining relaxation and prayer. Earlier this year at a workshop on healing in Venezuela when I had just finished giving a talk that had lasted more than an hour, I suggested that we pray for one or two people, then take a half-hour coffee break, and come back and pray for another hour before lunch, several people were somewhat shocked by the suggestion of stopping prayer for coffee. This was only the reaction of a couple of people, but it does show that they felt one activity (praying) was holy, and the other profane, and that I was stopping something holy in favor of another less-worthy activity.

depending on the guidance of the Spirit, on whether or not anything seems to be happening, and on the strength and energy of the participants.

In many ways I find it helps to think of soaking prayer as being like radiation or X-ray therapy. The longer the diseased area is held under the radiation of God's healing power, the more diseased cells are killed. At times you can even see a tumor or growth gradually disappear as you pray.

The problem, of course, with cobalt radiation is that healthy cells get killed, too; so the treatment sessions have to be fairly short so that the healthy tissues of the body are not too badly hurt. On the other hand, the wonderful thing about prayer is that there are no harmful side effects. You can pray as long as you want. The only limit imposed is our own strength, since prayer does take something out of us; so we have to set limits and rest.

This means that soaking prayer can be something we do at regular intervals; parents can pray for five minutes a day for their retarded child; or we can try praying once a week for 15 minutes with an arthritic friend. On the other hand, we can decide to take a long time in one chunk and make an all-out effort; for example, a small group may decide to spend a whole afternoon, or a whole day, praying for a friend who has multiple sclerosis.

If we are going to spend considerable time with a person, we should ordinarily have some indication—through a gift of knowledge or some other sign—that we should spend all that much time. Furthermore, if we pray too long with a person and nothing much happens, he naturally tends to feel guilty—as if he had failed to meet expectations. So, ordinarily, I only pray for a protracted time when something really *begins to happen* in a fairly short prayer for healing; this improvement indicates that we need to take more time to bring the healing to completion.

Now, sometimes what is begun in a short prayer—for example, a tumor starts to get smaller—may just continue happening for several hours after we have finished praying and the person has gone home. At other times the improvement only seems to go on as long as we keep praying.[5] I don't understand all this; I'm just sharing what I've seen, so that you will not limit the way that God works but will remain open to what seems to be called for with each person you pray with.

For instance in June, 1975, at the Oregon Camp Farthest Out (a kind of retreat) we began praying in a group for Bunni Determan, a lovely teenager who was encased in a neck brace because of a severe scoliosis (S-shaped curvature of the spine). Bunni's mother, a nurse, was part of the group and was able to tell after we had prayed for 10 minutes that a change had taken place. So we kept praying for two hours and by the end of that time most of the curvature at the top of the spine had been straightened out. The next two days the group, including many of Bunni's teenage friends, prayed some more— another hour each day—and by the end of the CFO Bunni's back seemed about 80% improved. And with continued prayer by her mother and her friends she is now out of her neck brace and is about 90% of the way to having a straight back (scoliosis is a condition that normally deteriorates and does not improve; the doctor's work is to prevent further deterioration from taking place from the weight of the body bearing down on the crooked spine).

Someone always asks why we have to spend so much time praying with people; they point out that Jesus usually healed with a word.[6] We could answer that even

[5] I saw a man I prayed for in Phoenix a year ago. He had bone problems in his heel and ankle that made it impossible for him to walk without pain. When we prayed a year ago all the pain left and he was able to run up and down for the first time in years without pain. When I saw him last week he told me the healing had lasted, but it remained at the point to which it had improved at that time; namely, the pain had gone and much mobility had returned. But now as we prayed last week, still more movement returned to the stiffened ankle. The longer we prayed the more movement there was; finally I had to stop because others were waiting, but he and his wife will continue to pray toward a complete healing.

[6] This is the kind of legalism that works such devastation in prayer groups and in Christianity in general.

Jesus had to pray twice with the one blind man (Mk 8:22-26), and then he encouraged us to persist in asking day and night. In addition to that, I can only say that I have found for myself that taking time in prayer on occasion is essential; and it works! If someone else has a more powerful healing ministry and can cure a severe chronic illness by a word, I'm all for that. Maybe healings work gradually through some of us, because the life of Jesus in us needs to grow stronger; maybe, at a future time, healing will take place more quickly. So I want to encourage those of you who perhaps are still beginners and who need to be encouraged to spend more time in healing prayer.

All I know is that not too many severe illnesses are instantly healed—even through the ministry of those who have an established ministry of those who have an established ministry of healing (I'm speaking here in terms of the percentage of instant healings of severe sickness compared to the number of people prayed for). Although I see many minor ailments very quickly healed through prayer, it's the long-term organic problems, such as a broken bone or a palpable tumor, that take the most time. Compared to the weeks and months spent in a hospital to get ourselves cured or even just improved, eight hours of prayer seems short indeed. And if a person has spent 20 years suffering through a developing case of rheumatoid arthritis, he or she will feel that being healed through six months of once-a-week soaking prayer is a short time indeed.

And it will be without pain and without thousands of dollars spent in fees and hospitalization. I just thank God when I see a friend healed, no matter how much time and energy we have spent, bent over in prayer.

3. Soaking Prayer: Two Cases

To give you a further idea of the different ways that soaking prayer works I would like to share the two cases of Lisa and Teresa.

The first, Lisa Scarbrough, has just begun, and I have no idea what eventually might happen. Perhaps nothing much more will happen; or quite the opposite, an extraordinary and complete healing may eventually take place. But these beginnings will give you an idea of how you sense that God may be calling you, or a group of people, to pray for a sick person over a prolonged period of time. At the time of this writing, Lisa is eight and a half years old. At the age of two and a half, Lisa was thought to have a brain tumor, but after two and a half years of testing, the doctors diagnosed it as a demyelinization of the nervous system. Over a period of six years, the disease progressed until she lost her speech, her sight and her muscle coordination. She was completely bedridden and had to be tube-fed. Her spine was severely curved, causing the left rib cage to protrude and the right leg to be approximately two inches shorter than the left leg.

After one week of intermittent soaking prayer her mother, Mrs. Elyse Scarbrough (of Dallas, Texas), sent me her journal, from which the following passages are excerpted:

Thursday, April 22, 1976
Father Dominic Tamburello, O.P., called and invited me to come with Lisa to the Mass that would end the Dominican priests' retreat at Bishop Lynch High School. After the Mass Father MacNutt, Father Tamburello and Bob Cavnar prayed with Lisa after anointing her with oil.

The base of her spine straightened about an inch. (We prayed about 10 minutes.) Father MacNutt offered to come to my house the next morning to pray again with Lisa.[1]

Friday Morning, April 23
Bob Cavnar drove Father MacNutt to my house on the way to the airport. Some of the members of my prayer group (St. Pius X, Dallas) were also present. We marked the curve of her spine with red ink to see it more clearly. After praying about 20 minutes the curvature of the spine moved inward about an inch, and the right leg came down about a quarter of an inch. Praise the Lord! Different members of the prayer group remained throughout the day with Lisa after Father and Bob Cavnar had to leave for the airport.

Friday Afternoon, April 23
That afternoon I noticed the right leg had come down some more—only a little bit. Friends continued to come and pray with Lisa throughout the evening. Lisa could lie *flat* on her stomach, whereas she couldn't before.

Saturday, April 24
Prayer group members continued to come. I noticed the spine in the neck area had straightened somewhat. Her neck was more limber. The rib cage on the left side of her chest protruded less.

Sunday, April 25
I took Lisa to the prayer meeting at Bishop Lynch. A man came over during the middle of the meeting and asked if he could pray with Lisa. I nodded my head.

Toward the end of the meeting we sang one round of "Alleluia, My Father." Bob Cavnar said that we were going to sing the song again, and during the singing we could meditate on anything we wanted to ask God for—big or small. I was thinking about Lisa putting her arms

---

[1] As mentioned in the last chapter this was the kind of situation, with several hundred people standing around at a late hour waiting for prayer, that it seemed best to pray for Lisa at some other time when we could really concentrate our prayer on her alone. Something happened to Lisa's spine that night to give us hope that more healing would take place, if we could just find another time and place to pray some more.

around my neck, and, without looking down at her, I reached over and placed my hand on her chest. My hand started quivering, and I felt a sensation of warmth, then heat. When I felt the heat my hand started tingling.

The man who had prayed with Lisa earlier during the meeting noticed—by my face, I guess—that something was happening. He came over and began to pray, laying his hand by mine on Lisa's chest.

I couldn't move my hand. I felt the area of the protruded rib cage get soft like putty; then it went flat. More people became aware that something was happening and began to come over and pray.... The man who had asked to pray with Lisa earlier came over and told me that when he first came in and sat down and saw Lisa, the Lord had told him that her name was "Lisha" and that he was to pray for her.... There was great jubilation that night!

Monday, April 26, 1976
A group of four of us from St. Pius X prayer group were praying with Lisa. I had my fingers at the back of Lisa's neck massaging it. Once again I felt heat and a tingling sensation in my fingers. Involuntarily I began rubbing her larnyx with my thumb. Later that day, I noticed the spine in the neck area had straightened completely.

Current: April 29, 1976
The curvature in Lisa's spine is still moving, but so gradually that it is not noticeable at the time it is happening. We are continuing a daily routine of prayer with members of St. Pius X prayer group. And Lisa has been receiving Communion daily since April 23.

As you can see, Lisa's story is a beautiful example of the power of prayer to gradually roll back what had been the steady progress of disease. A minimum effect of prayer would be to halt the progress of disease. A maximum effect would be for it to be more or less instantly healed. And somewhere in between is what we often see happen, as in the case of Lisa.

Also it is beautiful to see the interaction of Christian community in this prayer—and that the mother herself had a large part in it. They didn't have to wait for a well-known minister of healing to come to town again; instead, the dozens of people who prayed had a lively realization that Jesus is at work in his people as a body.

Another thing worth noting is that in this case, although there were many areas of Lisa's body affected, the healing that was taking place centered in the spine (which is where we had begun to pray). There is no record of the sight coming back[2] or the paralysis of the arms and legs being healed.

This kind of healing often begins in a particular area of the body. Perhaps it is in the area least affected by the disease; it makes sense to expect that life will first begin to return to those areas least deeply affected. Usually when I pray with someone I ask, after a time, if he or she feels anything happening. If they do feel something going on then I try to forward in prayer whatever it is that God is already doing. In *Healing* I describe the experience of Sister Avina, when we were all praying for her knee, when her face (we weren't even aware of the problem she had there) was healed. Jesus' principle of discernment was: "I do what I see the Father doing." So I try to find out, when possible, what it is that God is doing—or wants done— rather than to approach a sick person with my own prejudging notions of how God should work. Pray for a while and see if anything happens. If it does, continue praying along that line. (When nothing happens, you must learn to accept that, too, without necessarily feeling that you have failed, and without putting the sick person under a similar cloud of guilt.)

Teresa, the woman with the withered leg—The most remarkable example of healing through soaking prayer I have ever seen took place after a retreat we gave in the Diocese of Sonson—Rionegro, Colombia, South America, in February, 1975. Bishop Alphonso Uribe had invited me to give a retreat for priests there, and our team included Father Carlos Aldunate, S.J. (of Chile), Sister Jeanne Hill, O.P., Mrs. William Callaghan, and Alberto

---

[2] In a phone call last night a doctor from Texas informed me that her sight is now beginning to come back (Dec. 15, 1976).

del Corral as translator.[3] Although the retreat was for priests, other people heard about it and came onto the retreat grounds asking for prayer. So it was no surprise for me to find, after the last conference (around 4 p.m.), Mrs. Callaghan, Sister Jeanne and others praying for a young Colombian woman; they called me over to show me her deformed leg and told me that already something had happened—that the leg had grown an inch or more. So I joined them in their prayer. Talking to the 19-year-old woman, Teresa Patino, I found that she had stepped on a sharp object in a swamp when she was only five years old. Due to the lack of proper medical attention, an infection developed and then went to her bone and developed into osteomyelitis. As a result her right leg had been warped, as it were, from the knee down. It was about six inches shorter than the other leg and twisted as well. There also was a deep scar where an unsuccessful bone graft had been attempted.

As we prayed gently for two hours, the leg seemed to grow about an inch. About eight of us were praying, taking turns holding her leg (since kneeling down for several hours can be painful). The bishop himself prayed as part of the group.

Then we took a break for supper and came back to pray for another two hours that night. Again, it seemed that her leg grew still another inch. Also, the twisted leg was gradually straightening. You couldn't see it happen, because it was so gradual, but by comparing the length every 10 minutes or so, we could see the comparative change taking place.

The next day we gathered at Alberto del Corral's home in Medillin—again with Bishop Uribe—and prayed two more hours in the morning and two in the afternoon (prayer of this kind takes a lot out of you[4]). This day the

---

[3] His account of this healing is in the April, 1976, issue of *New Covenant*, pp. 26-28.

[4] Because this kind of prayer is work, some people tend to drop out over a course of time, even though results are taking place. People tend toward the instant and the spectacular. For this reason, families really need to learn how to pray for the chronically ill in their families. The Church has to teach more than acceptance and resignation.

leg seemed to grow another inch (it had grown about three inches the day before), so that by evening there was only about a two-inch difference between the two legs. Most remarkably, though, the right foot, which was flat and had no arch to speak of, grew and changed shape until the arch came in as in the normal foot. The toes of the deformed foot, which were about half the size of those on the other foot, also grew until they were almost the size of those on her normal foot. In a period of hours her toes on the right foot had nearly doubled in size!

Several other unusual developments occurred which helped us to understand better some of the factors we had already learned about healing. They had to do with the relation between bodily healing and spiritual healing. Twice we came to realize there was a need for a healing at the spiritual level; both realizations—one in the morning, one in the afternoon—came because the healing and the growth seemed to have stopped. After the first cessation we discovered that Teresa needed to forgive her mother for what had happened after the osteo had developed. Because her family was poor, Teresa's mother had to give Teresa up and board her with other people who could afford to get her the proper medical treatment. It was the only thing that could be done in the circumstances but to Teresa as a child it seemed like rejection. After we asked Teresa to forgive her mother and after praying for an inner healing of her feelings of rejection, Teresa's leg again started straightening and growing.

The second incident happened during the afternoon when the leg again seemed to stop growing (this was always hard to ascertain, since it could only be checked by comparative measurement over the course of perhaps half an hour). This time we found that a brother of Teresa's was severely injured in a wreck some years before and she had offered her crippled state to God if only he would spare her brother's life. So she was feeling guilty about the healing taking place, since it seemed to her like going back on a promise she had once made to God. Here Bishop Uribe stepped in to help by using his authority as God's representative to free her from the effects of any such vow. Once again her leg started to heal.

As that day of prayer ended we also noticed how the deep scar on her leg had grown closer to the surface and, except in two spots, it was not white instead of the purplish color it had been throughout its length when we started the day before. Since by now her right leg had grown enough to reach the ground (for years she had needed crutches because her right leg was too short to reach the ground), Teresa wanted to try walking for the first time since she was a child, but we told her to wait until she had checked it out with a doctor. Alberto offered to take her to a doctor and to form a team that would continue praying with her. Bishop Uribe, too, promised to stop by her home and pray with her once a week.

Since then her leg has continued to grow until there is only half an inch difference. at one session her foot made a turn until the scar that had formed a spiral down her leg became a straight line from the knee to the foot.

The group checked with a doctor who examined Teresa and said that the bone was still broken and weak and counseled against walking yet. Alberto describes the further developments:

Shortly after her visit to the doctor, a group gathered again with Bishop Uribe for further prayer. As we laid hands on Teresa we noticed that the place where the bone was broken was quite warm and the lump greatly reduced in size. We prayed for abmut two hours and finally Bishop Uribe asked Teresa to stretch her leg and foot, an act which always caused a great deal of pain. Hesitantly, Teresa stretched out her leg and as she did so, the bone stayed in place for the first time in years. She felt no pain or discomfort as she moved her leg. We were all quite joyful and thankful, for it seemed as if the bone had welded. However, we advised Teresa to see a doctor before using her leg. Several days later she saw not one but two doctors, both of whom confirmed that her bone had welded.[5]

Now, for the first time in 14 years, Teresa is walking again.

---

[5] *New Covenant* magazine, April, 1976, p. 27.

It's impossible to calculate exactly how many hours of soaking prayer went into this extraordinarily healing. Nor how many people prayed. And there is still need for more prayer for the leg still needs more healing. But most of the healing, which required that her leg and foot grow and straighten and be mended—when the doctors had given up hope of any further improvement taking place—has now taken place.

Again—it's impossible to say for sure—I don't think any of Teresa's healing would have taken place if we hadn't learned something about the time element required in praying for healing, nor if there hadn't been friends willing to spend hours gathered around Teresa in prayer. To see changes take place in a deformed leg like Teresa's is exciting; to see the tears of gratitude in her eyes as she felt her leg strengthen is all the human reward anyone would ever need after spending hours praying with her.

But when you start praying, you never know—unless God reveals it—how much might happen, or not happen. And it's hard work—at times, exhausting. No wonder Jesus referred to his healings as "works"—"The works I do in my Father's name are my witness" (Jn 10:25), rather than as "miracles."

Seeing the effects of soaking prayer has given me a whole new outlook on healing. It used to be that when I passed a cripple I would wonder if prayer would heal him, but at the same time I would feel that the chances of a cure—although possible were slim. Now when I see a cripple I just wonder if he could not be cured, or at least dramatically improved, if there were only someone who could take the time to sit beside him and pray.

4. Degrees of Improvement

The time element in prayer often results in sick people being improved rather than completely healed, either because we haven't spent enough time praying with them or because we don't have enough spiritual power or resources to completely vanquish the illness. Likewise, we have found that there are corresponding plateaus of healing, like steps. (If a person reaches a certain level of healing, that does not necessarily mean that he or she will move on to the next or be completely healed.) For those who pray for healing, it is important to know about the existence of these levels:

1) *Cessation of pain:*

Often the pain stops when we pray for people who are suffering. Sometimes this is the beginning of a healing or the sign that a healing is taking place, but just because the person you are praying with tells you that the pain has gone away doesn't always mean that he or she is healed. I have prayed for several terminal cancer patients whose pain left to such an extent that they no longer needed painkillers. Yet, they died of the cancer. When this alleviation of pain occurs, we can count this as a great blessing for which we praise God without pretending to understand why the healing did not progress further.

2) *Removal of side effects of treatment:*

As we know, most medicines have undesirable side effects that unbalance or tear down the body, even while they help the body heal itself. One of the remarkable things we have seen take place in the past year is that

29

several people we have prayed for who were undergoing chemotherapy or radiation treatment did not experience the ordinary adverse side effects. One little girl we were praying for who had cancer and was undergoing chemotherapy suffered none of the usual lassitude caused by this kind of treatment and whenever her blood count would become imbalanced, we would pray for her and she was spared the scheduled blood transfusion. Two other ministers of healing, whom I know very well and trust, tell me of cancer patients they have prayed for with a prayer of protection. They were spared the usual harmful side effects, such as having their hair fall out.[1]

From all this we learn to pray for protection from any adverse side effects of the medicine prescribed by doctors for the patients we pray for. One nurse I know begins her work at the hospital by taking all the medicines she is going to pass out during the day and then says a prayer over the medicine asking God to work through the medicine a) to empower it with its proper healing effect, and b) to inhibit any side effects harmful to the patients. This is modern updating of the ancient Church practice of

---

[1] The following is from a letter I recently received:

... I'm 40 years old and the mother of four children. Five years ago I had a mastectomy, and about a year and a half ago the doctors discovered that the cancer had spread to my liver and there were a few "specks" in my stomach. They shook their heads and sent me home after taking out my ovaries, saying in a few weeks I could start on chemotherapy. . . .

When I went back to my family doctor we had a long talk about healing and when I left he wrote on his prescription pad: *Healing* by Father MacNutt . . . When I would become afraid after that I would read "God loves you, he wants to help you, have faith, he *will heal you*," etc. . . . We found out that our parish was having prayer meetings. My husband took me over and that first night he stood up, explained my situation, and begged for help. The whole community prayed for me. My husband and children also laid hands on me at home and we prayed our heads off.

Well, first we prayed that I wouldn't get sick from the chemotherapy; I DIDN'T. Then that my hair wouldn't fall out; IT DIDN'T. And, of course, praying all the time that Jesus would heal me of this cancer. The last verification I've had was when the doctor took another liver scan, and he said it showed the tumor to be much, much smaller. . .

blessing oil, which in the early Christian era was the universal medicine—as in the story of the Good Samaritan who took the beaten traveler "and bandaged his wounds, pouring oil and wine on them" (Lk 11:34). The special blessing for oil was not a superstitious settling on the one element, oil, but was simply the Church taking the natural medicine of that era and praying for it to be empowered to have its natural effect and work even beyond that capacity as God's chosen instrument of healing.

3) *Stabilization of sickness without full healing:*

At times, it seems that our prayer has just enough power to stop the sickness in its tracks, but not to overcome and remove it altogether. A good example of this would be cancer; where the growth of the cancer is arrested but not removed. Just recently I prayed again with a friend who has multiple sclerosis; the first time we prayed was two years ago and, since then, he has had no more attacks—a remarkable thing medically. Yet the M.S. remains, in an arrested state. The last time we prayed (last month) nothing discernible happened with the M.S., and yet, two small skin cancers on his face (that I wasn't praying for) withered up and fell off the next morning—which was something his doctor had never seen in his practice.

Many marvelous spiritual developments have taken place in his life and in his marriage—far more important than the healing of the M.S.—and a great blessing has taken place: the cycle of M.S. attacks has been broken. Yet the M.S. lingers on in its arrested state.

4) *Return of physical function without healing of the illness:*

In my experience, there are a fair number of healings that take place wherein the injured person can now walk, or move his arm, or hear, or whatever, much to the surprise of the doctor, for nothing (or not that much) has changed physically that would account for the change in bodily function.

An example of this is the story of Richard Appleby of Charleston, South Carolina:

In November, 1973, I represented my pastor at a three-day seminar on the charismatic movement. At that time I didn't know anything about the renewal. In fact, I only went to the conference for the sake of my pastor.

One of the first speakers was Father Francis MacNutt, a Dominican priest active in the movement. He talked about speaking in tongues, the laying on of hands and healing in the modern Church. Coming from a Catholic priest, this surprised me. Although I was very skeptical, I began to pay closer attention.

That evening Father MacNutt led prayer for healing. I decided to tell him about my hip. About 14 years ago I developed a kink in my side, accompanied by a sharp pain. It gradually got worse and kept me awake at night. A specialist examined me, took X-rays, and discovered that my right hip was deteriorating. He said that the deterioration would progress, the pain intensify, and eventually I'd need a wheelchair or an operation. He added that the operation succeeded only 50 percent of the time.

I told Father MacNutt and he asked me to come forward and sit in the chair. He lifted my legs and noticed that one leg was about three inches shorter than the other. As he lowered my feet to the floor, he asked those close by to lay hands on me and pray. After a couple of minutes we stopped praying, and I heard a small gasp from a couple of people. Father MacNutt said, "Well, we've gained about an inch. Let's keep praying." Suddenly I felt a tingling sensation in my right leg and in the right lower side of my stomach. Then I felt a great warmth come over my hip. We stopped praying, took another look and Father MacNutt said, "We've gained another inch. Let's keep praying." By this time we were all praying as loudly as we could. Finally, Father MacNutt said, "Well, it looks to me as though both legs are the same length." Everyone in the hall praised God. I stood up and put my right foot on the floor perfectly for the first time in five years. I walked as steadily as I used to, completely free from pain. Everyone crowded around, congratulating me and thanking God.

In a daze I returned to my room, went to sleep, and the next thing I knew it was seven a.m. I had slept through the night for the first time in over five years! I wondered if the healing had been a dream. I quickly got out of bed, and when both feet hit the floor evenly I knew I had been healed.

When I got home I went to the same specialist. He took new X-rays, compared them to the old ones, and said that there was no difference in the bone structure. However, he couldn't explain the lengthening of my leg and my freedom from pain. I told him that the Lord had healed me. And he has. Jesus has set me free.[2]

5) *True bodily healing:*

This can be in all degrees, from just a little bit, all the way to a total healing.

Because of the diversity of these levels of improvement, we need to be sensitive and not proclaim that a total healing has taken place when a person says he no longer feels pain or when some real improvement has taken place.

On the other hand, just because total healing hasn't taken place does not mean that God has not acted to heal: we should be ready to praise him for all the levels of healing that are steps on the way to perfect life and wholeness.

You may be wondering why I am setting down all these distinctions about levels of healing—doesn't it burden us with a lot of intellectual baggage? I think it should do quite the opposite: it should set us free. All these distinctions indicate the variety of ways that God works. I constantly receive letters from people who ask what to do about persons in their prayer groups who have learned a *few* principles about praying for healing and who go around applying these principles in an absolute, legalistic, insensitive fashion. Because some people seem to be healed through their ministry, they see this as justifying their particular understanding of what they do. But it's quite possible for them to help some people and still have

---

[2] *New Covenant* magazine, Vol. 4, No. 5 (Nov. 1974), p. 28.

a very faulty notion of what they are doing, which in turn will spiritually and psychologically harm those they pray for.

Just to know that healing is a mystery—that it's complicated and not all that simple—should free us from any need to give simplistic answers to people who wonder why they are not totally healed. To know how complex healing is helps us to rely more upon God's light, to seek real discernment, and to let go of simplified solutions. The very people who boast of knowing no theology, but only the word of God, are the very ones who are most likely to impose their own impoverished theology (which they may call "discernment") upon the hapless sick person who is just desperate enough at that point to accept anything proposed with absolute authority.

To know about these levels actually should free us from intellectualism as well as fundamentalism and release us to be part of the *mystery* of God's healing love.

5. The Levels of Divine Activity

Healings also differ in the extent to which they demonstrate clearly the supernatural intervention of God. At times it is obvious, and "provable," that healings are absolutely beyond the curative powers of nature. These healings are visibly *supernatural* in origin. But at other times God chooses to work less visibly; he accomplishes the healing by working through *natural* causes.

PROBLEMS WITH CLAIMING MIRACLES

Two years ago several of us involved in the charismatic renewal visited Lourdes to participate in a two-day dialogue with the doctors and chaplains. Abbe Rene Laurentin, O.S.B., was the person who brought us all together and chaired the meeting. We all found it mutually beneficial; Dr. Theodore Mangiapan and the other doctors on the staff at Lourdes impressed upon us the need for persons in the charismatic renewal to be more sparing in talking about miracles, since the Medical Bureau at Lourdes has always tried to be very careful before ever proclaiming any cure miraculous. In the four years, in fact, previous to our meeting (May, 1975), the doctors had not sent up a single case to the International Board to be certified as miraculous, and only some 62 cures had met the rigid criteria for the miraculous in the more than 100 years of the Medical Bureau's existence at Lourdes.

Yet the doctors themselves were frustrated. Although they could see consistent evidence of God's healing power, most of these cures could not be proven as absolutely beyond the natural curative power of nature. They had records of some 4,000 "healings" that were beyond the limits of their medical knowledge to explain, but these healings had still failed to measure up to one or another of the rigid norms of proof the Catholic Church had set up. The doctors were impatient because they had to spend so much time trying to document cures, while theologians were questioning the validity of the distinction between the natural and supernatural. By the eye of faith, they could see for themselves the evidence of God's healing power. They were asking if their talents couldn't be put to more use than documenting only one miraculous cure every three or four years.

If the Medical Bureau at Lourdes, with all its examinations and X-rays, has difficulty coming up with proof that a cure is beyond natural possibilities, I experience even more difficulty in presenting healing to a scientific audience. I have had many excellent, productive meetings with groups of doctors, but still some think I am trying to prove that each case of healing which takes place through our prayer is miraculous. In most cases you can "prove" nothing absolutely. It's much more like an inductive argument: if you pray for a large number of people you will see so much physical improvement and healing take place (in addition to the subjective impressions of heat, or bones shifting around, or pain leaving) that you will probably receive an overwhelming impression (as I have) that the power of God is really at work, even though you can't prove it by any one instance.

Once, when I described to a group of doctors how I prayed and a tumor disappeared within an hour, one doctor responded that I couldn't prove that the prayer was what *caused* the tumor to go down. All I could legitimately claim was that I prayed and *after* that the tumor disappeared. And *he was right*.

It is only after you have seen such things happen frequently after prayer that you can offer some kind of inductive argument. The old adage here holds true: For the believer no argument is necessary; for the unbeliever no argument will prove sufficient.

There are several ways in which some line of proof could be set up, since scientists continue to be interested in finding evidence as to the value of prayer, and I suggest that a better way than the traditional one (proving the single dramatic miraculous healing) would be to take two similar groups of patients suffering from a particular disease. Pray with one group for healing, and compare the results with the other, the control group. I suspect that a significant difference would be found in these two groups.

I respect the attempts of some Christian doctors or scientists to prove to the scientific community the reality of God's healing power.[1] But, in a way, talking about miracles and their proof obscures what we are trying to do, because so little of what is accomplished through prayer can be proven in a scientific way. How can we show that most healings through prayer are beyond the powers of nature? Most are not!

Charismatic groups should respect the problems that doctors and theologians have with their often too casual claims of miraculous healings. It isn't that the doctors and theologians lack faith. It's just that their professions demand precision, and they are appalled by the kind of absolute, unsubstantiated claims of healing made at prayer meetings.[2] Theologians and churchmen, in particular, are sensitive to quackery. The general

---

[1] As Dr. H. Richard Casdorph does in *Miracles* (Plainfield, N.J.; Logos, 1976) in which he shows X-rays and gives medical reports on cures that had taken place through prayer mostly in Kathryn Kuhlman services.

[2] Dr. William Nolen, for example, in his critical appraisal, *Healing: A Doctor in Search of a Miracle* (New York; Random House, © 1974) investigates only one Christian healer, Kathryn Kuhlman, who tried to help him out by sending him a letter with references of patients who were healed. "Her letter was very friendly but the line that interested me most was this: 'What I tried to do (referring to the list of patients) was give you a variety, and diseases that could not possibly have been psychosomatic.' When I looked at the list I found that two-thirds of the patients suffered from diseases such as multiple sclerosis, rheumatoid arthritis, paralysis (no cause listed), loss of sight, and allergies, in all of which the psyche often plays a major and dominant role. It was apparent from her letter that Miss Kuhlman knew very little next to nothing about psychosomatic illness" (p. 100).

impression in the scientific community is that so-called "healings" are usually the result of autosuggestion among simple people worked over by a high-powered evangelist.

LEVELS OF HEALING

To put all this in perspective, I think it will help to keep in mind that there are several levels of healing. These distinctions should help those engaged in the ministry of prayer-for-healing, as well as those in the scientific community who are trying to understand what we are doing when we pray for healing.[3] Following is a list of some forces at work when we pray for physical healing. Healing may take place

1. *Through Purely Natural Forces Released in Prayer:*

Those involved in the ministry of healing need have no difficulty in admitting that some of the cures attributed to prayer may be caused by

a. *the power of suggestion.* Especially at prayer meetings where emotion is high, some diseases are notoriously susceptible of improvement, when there is a strong desire for healing on the part of the sick person, coupled with a powerful positive suggestion on the part of the evangelist. A multiple sclerosis patient, for instance, upon receiving a great emotional lift in a meeting, may be able to stand up and walk. The next day the person may be back in the wheelchair.

It is also possible that a person may be competely cured through strong suggestion, which can come in prayer.

b. *Christian love.* When a sick person experiences

---

[3] In what follows, theologians will note that, although I find God working in the entirety of the natural and human order, I see no difficulty in his working more directly in a "supernatural" way. I do not see this as "interfering," as some theologians do. It's simply that the traditional way of looking at creation and at the miraculous seems to concur with what I find in experience. I do not believe in a two-tiered universe, in which one level is labeled natural and the other supernatural. God is at work in every aspect of creation. Still, he seems to act more directly at some times than others, the forces of nature.

Christian love in a group, this love has a curative power of its own. This power to heal can be considerable!

c. *laying on of hands.* Studies done at the New York University School of Nursing indicate that there may be some kind of *natural* curative effect when people lay their hands on a patient with the intent of healing.

As long as we recognize that God works in his creation, we need not be threatened by recognizing that some cures at prayer meetings are caused by suggestion or other such forces. On the other hand, critics of the ministry of healing, such as Dr. William Nolen, have not disproven the effectiveness of prayer when they have shown that many of the healings claimed at Kathryn Kuhlman's services could be attributed to suggestion or to psychosomatic influences.

2. *Through Spiritual or Emotional Healing:*

Because of the close interrelationship between our bodies and our emotional and spiritual health, some physical sicknesses clear up when the roots of anxiety or bitterness are removed through a ministry of prayer. If arthritis, for instance, is related, in a particular person, to pent-up anger and this anger is released through forgiving someone or through inner healing, the arthritis may clear up dramatically.

Again, critics with a proof-mentality may say that this was *only* the cure of a psychosomatic problem. Yet a psychosomatic cure is a real cure. Doctors often have less success curing psychosomatic problems (e.g., curing rheumatoid arthritis if the arthritis is caused by stress) than they have curing purely bodily sickness (e.g., helping a broken arm heal). If Christian ministry and prayer can effect this type of psychosomatic cure they will have made a notable contribution to present-day medicine.

3. *Through the Natural Recuperative Forces of the Body Speeded Up by Prayer:*

To me this seems to be the most common type of healing by prayer. Of its very nature it cannot be proven, because the cure is accomplished through the natural

39

recuperative forces in the body. Yet, healing might not have taken place at all or might not have happened so fast, if the prayer had not somehow stimulated and quickened the sick person's body.

At the most mundane level we observe this when we pray for a cold to be healed, and the cold disappears much faster than we would ordinarily expect. At a more difficult level we see it when we pray for a cancer patient who is already receiving radiation treatment, and the cancer is arrested and then healed. How can we tell whether the healing was directly from God or through the processes of nature, aided by medical treatments destroying the cancer cells? That is a question often asked—a question which is, in a way, a false question, because the power of God can surely improve or aid the natural healing process and work *through it and not apart from it*. The healing takes place through nature—which is God's creation—but in a sense is beyond the ordinary because the natural recuperative forces have been implemented and increased through prayer.

We cannot produce direct evidence for this in any given instance, but after praying for thousands of people I have no doubt myself about how God's healing power amplifies the healing power of nature, because of the *rapidity* of the healings that regularly take place. It may happen, for example, that a person who is scheduled for a two-week stay in a hospital following an operation is ready to leave the hospital after a mere four-day recovery.

4. *Through Natural Forces, But in a Manner Out of the Ordinary:*

A good example of this is the healing of scoliosis (S-shape curvature of the spine). At times, I have seen this take place in a matter of minutes; at other times, in case of severe curvature, the prayer has taken hours, or even months, but without surgery or manipulation.

Suppose there is a girl who has been in a body brace to protect her spine from further deterioration (because of the weight of the body bearing down on the bent spine). As we pray we may find the spine gradually moving and straightening under our hands. From time to time there may be a cracking sound as a vertebra snaps into place. All this is happening without any pressure being applied. What is the force that is moving things back into alignment and holding them there? It is certainly not a process that seems normally to take place in the doctor's office (although changes in the spine can, of course, be effected through manipulation, selected exercises or surgery).

Sometimes we pray over a tumor and it starts to disappear before our very eyes. The disappearance of the growth can, of course, be brought about by medical means, but upon occasion an inoperable tumor will disappear as we pray—or after we pray—sometimes in a matter of minutes. Again, it is often difficult to prove anything miraculous has taken place in this kind of healing, even when we have the medical records.

Sometimes the speed at which a terminal cancer is healed or something in the *manner* of the cure could be termed miraculous. A good example of this is contained in the following account of a cure of spider cancer (a letter from Mr. Harold Beckman, Phoenix, Arizona):

Dear Mom and Dad,

I want to get a note off to you, Mom and Dad, before the holidays so we can all share in a thanksgiving in celebrating the birth of Our Lord and Savior, Jesus Christ....

My problems as you know started back in 1965 when my back was crushed and I was sent to the hospital. Two surgeries were performed in 13 days for the removal of two crushed discs, one at each surgery.

I was able to go home after the second operation, only to have a huge abscess develop and had to return to the hospital again. In a couple of weeks this healed and in a couple of months I was able to return to work.

The stay at work was short-lived when four tumors appeared on my lower back with intense pain. This required more surgery to remove these tumors.

It was shortly after this we received the grim truth that I had developed the strange disease called arachnoiditis (a rare disease) and that the lining of the durasac in my lower back had been torn in three or possibly four places, allowing the spinal fluid to escape, not all but a significant portion of it.

This required six months of complete bed rest and I had to be in a lower Fowler position all that time; I wasn't even able to turn over in bed day and night.

When the six months were up, things were no better so then we left for the Mayo Clinic where two more surgeries were performed, but still things kept deteriorating.

After several months and no cure we decided to go to the University of Iowa only to have Mayo Clinic's determination verified and was told I would have to spend the rest of my life in bed with the exception of a few hours up in a wheelchair each day.

Both Mayo Clinic and University of Iowa recommended brain surgery to eliminate the severe pain—that made 13 major operations up to this time.

After this we returned to Phoenix to have this surgery done. The first surgery of the brain helped to relieve the pain in the right side but the second brain surgery made the back pain more severe.

It was by this time a huge tumor had developed in my right lung, collapsing it and tearing it away from the chest wall. It required more surgery to remove this tumor and fuse the lung back to the chest wall. There was a total of 16 tumors removed by then.

The latest suffering was closely followed by seizures and more suffering for my whole family (my wife and six children) because I had to be placed in a nursing home and on heavy medication to control the seizures and pain. This continued for the past three years and it was in the last six months of my stay in the nursing home that Our Lord Jesus Christ became very live and exciting in our lives.

My beautiful family belonged to a prayer group and had gone to a Life in the Spirit Seminar and received the baptism of the Holy Spirit. Later on, leaders from their prayer group started a prayer group at the nursing home. This I attended—then began a Life in the Spirit Seminar. In the fourth week of the seminar it still wasn't clear to me whether or not to let myself be baptized in the Spirit without further study and as I lay in bed that night praying decided I would be baptized the next week.

The baptism was to be on Tuesday but on Monday evening I had the worst seizure I had ever had come on me. It lasted longer than any I had ever had. I was always very shook after these seizures and didn't want to see anyone or talk to anyone. I don't know where I got the strength to call my wife to tell her I didn't want any visitors. Well, three men from her prayer group came anyway unbeknown to each other.

One was an ordained deacon. He brought Communion and they asked me if I wanted to be baptized in the Holy Spirit and wanted them to pray over me. All I could say was "please do." This was the most exciting time in my life—Praise God.

I felt like in the front of my head a large ball was growing and I got so very hot—then I felt like water was surging through my body. I then saw Jesus on the foot of my bed washing me down, all this went away and then I felt water running out of my feet.

The men stopped praying and quietly left and instead of going into a painful deep sleep like after all the other seizures I became wide awake and sat up in bed. I just got terribly excited and started praising God and at the same time wondering what had happened.

It was about eleven in the evening when it began to unfold. It started with my bladder that had been paralyzed for months. The catheter started to pain something terrible to the point of not being able to stand it. The nurse removed the catheter and in a short time my bladder started to function normally. (I was to go back to the hospital in 10 days and have my bladder and bowels put externally.) Again I praised God.

Now I knew the Lord's power was upon me. I just couldn't sleep that night and when daylight came I got in my wheelchair and went into the bathroom. I stood up and just knew I was healed the pain was gone completely. The tears began to flow and continued for three days before I realized they were tears of joy.

This was the end of nine long years of suffering for my wonderful, loving wife, Barbara, my children and myself. When we came back from Mayo Clinic and Iowa City we were told that my disease was terminal and was arachnoiditis or spider cancer, a more recent name, but God knew better.

Today I feel wonderful. I take no medicine of any kind (and was on a tremendous amount of high-potency drugs for the past nine years). I have no bladder or bowel trouble, no seizures and didn't notice until I came home that the big toe on my right foot which had bad infection in it and never would heal was completely healed now.

Also by the time the nine full years were up I had 16 major surgeries; my vision was so impaired that I qualified and had to utilize the National Blind Foundation so that I could "hear" various news magazines, books, records, etc. I had lost all feeling from my chest area down and could not be moved without going into a seizure. I had spent the last three years in a nursing home in connection with a hospital.

In October I was examined by a neurologist who has confirmed the fact that I have had a miracle.

There is no scar tissue which was causing the seizures where they did the brain surgery. My back is perfect, my bowels and bladder are, too, and my spinal cord has fluid in it again, so I can truly say, "He touched me." Praise be to God.

5. *Through Preternatural Forces:*

For those who have no experience in praying for exorcism or deliverance, it may seem inappropriate to discuss demonic influence in healing, but my experience (and study) leads me to believe that evil spirits exist, that they can cause sickness, and that they can also heal by removing the sickness they cause. In most nations and cultures—including the United States—there are witches or spiritualists who claim to curse and also to heal. (In Venezuela, for example, the most prevalent form of spiritual healing is through devotion to the spirit of a dead witch whose followers claim the power to heal.)

I see no reason to deny that there is a power in spiritualism that works. The pastoral practice of the Catholic Church has always accepted the power of spirits as a real force in human affairs, although recent times have seen the ministry of deliverance played down in the

Church, even as it has been played up on the motion picture screen.

Visiting in Bogota, Colombia, I ran across an interesting case in which a mother—living in a Christian community, by the way—took her son, who had fallen prey to a sudden, mysterious illness, down the street to see a spiritualist healer. Upon paying her cash fee the spiritualist told this mother that her next-door neighbor, in a fit of anger, had asked this same spiritualist to put a curse on the boy. It was at that time the boy fell sick. The spiritualist agreed to remove the curse and to pray for healing; after this the boy became well again. Ironically, the spiritualist was paid twice: once for imposing sickness, once for removing it. And even more ironically, all these individuals were nominally Christian, including the spiritualist.

Healing of this kind should, of course, come through a form of deliverance prayer said by a Christian, but freedom from sickness can also come through the same demonic force that originally imposed it. This may sound very primitive and scientifically unsupportable to many readers, but the simple people in most countries of the world that I have visited have a strong belief in the reality of these preternatural forces. Even Christians will seek the help of their *curandero*, or whatever the healer is called in their culture, if the Christian bishops, priests and ministers do not believe in praying for healing. My own experience leads me to a firm conviction in the reality of the demonic realm and of its power to curse and to heal. These powers are ultimately destructive and enslaving; it is important to recognize them, rather than to deny them, and to learn to apply the power of the Holy Spirit in healing, so that sick people will not be driven to seek help from an alien and dangerous source.

6. *Through a Creative Act of God—A Miracle in the Strict Sense:*

This is the rarest type of healing that takes place and is the only one susceptible of proof   provided we have all the evidence. This kind of creative act, where nature has no known capability of acting, is the most difficult to believe—especially for those scientifically trained to seek a rational physical cause for every effect. When I pray for a sick person in whom some kind of natural power can be quickened (for instance, a person with cataracts) I have little difficulty believing in the efficacy of my prayer. I am not too surprised if a person with cataracts finds that his or her vision becomes more clear—or completely clear— after we have prayed. I can visualize the cloudiness and the unnatural growth being dissolved in a natural way. But when I pray for someone like a blind person who has no eye at all in the socket and realize that only a new creation of some kind can enable that person to see, then I cannot afford to think too long about how this cure might take place. I also know that such cures or miracles—it's not really a "healing," is it?[4]—are rare; and I am surprised when they take place.

But the point is, they do take place. In *Healing*, I tell the story of the three Indians who told about their teeth being filled through prayer. That is a difficult story for most people to accept; nevertheless, since writing about that event, I have met more people who have experienced the filling of teeth[5] through prayer, and I have even

---

[4] In I Cor 12: 9-10, St. Paul distinguishes between the gift of *healing* and the power of working *miracles*. It's not possible to know exactly what Paul meant by miracles as distinct from healing, but he may have had in mind some kind of creation, such as we speak of here.

[5] One such interesting account comes from a woman who told me the following story when I met her at the Presbyterian Charismatic Conference in 1974. I asked her to set it down in a letter and here is what she wrote:

As for my teeth this goes back to the time you spoke at Oral Roberts University. You spoke about your visit to Blue Cloud Abbey and the Indian woman who had an experience with her teeth being filled. One day, probably six months later, the thought seemed to persist to have my husband pray for my teeth. I met him at work and asked him to pray. He wasn't interested and brushed the idea away. That evening I asked him again, and still no interest. Finally when he was in bed I remember telling him it was his last chance to pray. He didn't have the faith for this, but just to get rid of me, I guess, he prayed. I went into our living room and prayed in the Spirit and took God at his word in Psalm 81:10. I hated not to trust, but I

discovered a book on the subject.[6]

In my own ministry, I have never seen this particular kind of cure take place (although I have once seen teeth straightened through prayer), but I have no reason to doubt that it can and has taken place.

The reaction to this kind of testimony, however, is usually incredulity, because this type of healing activity does not fit into the world view of many contemporary theologians.

There are other healings that seem to be of this creative nature. Teresa, the 19-year-old girl from Colombia whose leg was lengthened about six inches and straightened, whose case was mentioned earlier, seems to be such a case. Occasionally there are cases of nerve damage being repaired, which does not happen in the ordinary course of nature.

If all the above seems a little complicated, that's because it is often difficult to try to gain an intellectual understanding of the manifold ways in which God works. This chapter does indicate several important things for everyone in the healing ministry to keep in mind:

1. *We should not be too insistent on claiming that a miracle has taken place.*

Often it is evident to everyone who has been involved that God has been at work in a prayer for healing and we can praise him for the extraordinary cure we have witnessed. Yet, to talk about a miracle to a group of people from a scientific background may not satisfy them

---

finally went into the bathroom to see and, sure enough, the Lord had filled two teeth. I knew that if God could create the earth with all its gold and silver, it wouldn't be too much to fill my teeth.

This account was verified by her pastor who wrote: "I have read her letter to you and can vouch for and verify that what she says is accurate."

[6] *Can God Fill Teeth?* by Daniel W. Fry (Lakemont, Ga., CSA Press, 1970). This is an intriguing book about the ministry of Rev. Willard Fuller in whose ministry it is claimed that "over one thousand people a year since 1960" have received gold, silver or porcelain fillings and about one hundred have received completely whole teeth. I have never met Rev. Fuller or been to one of his meetings, but I found this book a challenging one to read.

at all and may turn them off, because of our own sloppy terminology. Jesus himself did not often use the word "miracle" to describe his healings; the Gospel writers usually speak in terms of his "works," or "acts of power" or "signs." Similarly, I think we can speak in terms of "healings" taking place and can use the word "miracle" more sparingly and only when we have evidence that healing has taken place beyond the ordinary course of nature.

2. *More and less:*

Just as we have seen that there are degrees of more or less in many areas of the healing ministry, so I believe there are degrees of more or less direct and obvious involvement of God's power in healing. Nevertheless, seeing God's love at work, working through a natural process and speeding it up, is just as beautiful a thing as seeing a real creative miracle. It is not as startling but, with the eyes of faith, we should be able to praise God for the ways in which he works through a creation quickened by our love and prayer: the more direct involvement by God in true miracles, *as we see it*, may not be truly more at all; he is equally at work in the quiet processes of the nature he has created and which he continues to sustain: as Paul said, "Yet in fact he is not far from any of us, since it is in him that we live, and move, and exist..." (Acts 17:28).

3. *Proving that miracles take place is important but secondary:*

Since the limits of what nature can accomplish are so uncertain (e.g., is the healing of multiple sclerosis, attested over a lengthy period of time, a miracle that can only be explained by God's power?), it is becoming increasingly difficult to say that something is beyond the limits of the natural order.

Furthermore, most of the healings that take place have multiple causes so that one can't often tell whether prayer was the basic source of healing, or medical attention, or a spontaneous remission (as in a cancer patient who recovers after receiving prayer and chemotherapy). It's usually impossible to show which factors were at work in any kind of scientific way.

Yet, if you are actively involved in the healing ministry, you will see so many healings take place that you won't have any practical doubts about God's powerful activity when you pray. The explanations and proofs are needed for those not involved in the healing ministry, really. It's a mistake for us to center our thoughts on what is or what is not a miracle, since so much of what happens is a marvelous combined working of God's creative power in and through and with his own creation.

Why feel threatened when a doctor says that the healing we claimed for God in the prayer meeting was of a psychosomatic illness and our prayer merely touched the subconscious of the person and, so, touched off a psychological process releasing an apparent bodily healing? This, too, is a kind of healing. If 80 percent of illness is psychosomatic in origin, as some doctors claim, then 80 percent of bodily healings should primarily involve a healing of the psyche, the emotions. That doesn't take away from the glory of God; the emotional healing is as real as the physical. And for all our knowledge of psychosomatic medicine, how many of these illnesses are actually cured by medicine? Are ulcers, for instance, cured any more easily than broken bones? On the contrary, the purely physical, the broken bones are often more readily healed than the psychosomatic ulcers. If prayer can help cure ulcers, a doctor is not downgrading prayer by pointing out that the patient's basic problem was worry and not an ulcerated stomach lining. To say that the sickness was *only* emotional and not physical disproves nothing of the power of prayer; emotional sickness is real sickness and is often harder to heal than bodily injury. (It might be more accurate to be thankful that someone's illness is *only physical*!)

It is all God's world—and God is at work in marvelous and manifold ways. The more ways we see God at work, the more we sense the beauty and mystery of it all and the more we can praise him.

6. The Story of Roell: The Difficulty of Proof

Recently an account appeared in the St. Louis Archdiocesan Catholic paper which beautifully illustrates what I spoke about in the last chapter: the marvelous effect of prayer that touches everyone concerned with a healing, together with the impossibility of proving anything scientifically. The proof is of its nature impossible in this kind of case, no matter how much evidence we garner, but that is almost beside the point. There are many other teachings that you will surely notice as you read this heartening story—notably the benefit of continued, soaking prayer. I wish I knew at what point Roell was healed: Was it at the first prayer or did it require all those months of prayer? We will never know.

But here is her story.[1]

They do not claim that a miracle has occurred. However, the parents of four-year-old Roell Ann Schmidt of St. Roch Parish here firmly believe that God cured their daughter of cancer.

Moreover, they believe that God acted in response to very specific prayers for healing, as offered weekly by Catholics who themselves firmly believe in the power of prayer to heal.

Their belief is buttressed by the physicians and surgeons from St. Louis Children's Hospital who decline to take credit for what appears to be a permanent cure of cancer—a cancer that is 95 percent fatal in most similar cases.

---

[1] Under the title, "Child's Cure Causes Thanksgiving After Intense Prayer, Therapy," by Robert J. Byrne in the *St. Louis Review*, Oct. 15, 1976, Section 2, p. 1.

To give credit where credit is due, the Schmidts arranged a public Mass of Thanksgiving for the healing of Roell Ann on Aug. 23 at St. Roch Church... with Msgr. Robert M. Peet, pastor, as principal concelebrant. ...Some 80 persons attended, most of them persons who had been praying fervently for Roell's recovery for nearly a year. Because such a Mass of Thanksgiving is relatively rare, and because of the believed significance of prayer in Roell's apparent cure, Mr. and Mrs. Schmidt agreed to explain, in detail, to the *St. Louis Review*, the circumstances of their daughter's illness, her treatment, their recourse to prayer and the girl's apparent cure.

It should be noted that these are the details of one particular case. They are related because of a growing interest in the numbers of Catholics in prayer groups who are praying for—and often receiving—cures of physical and emotional illnesses. Church authorities here have not taken any official stand—one way or the other—about the Schmidts.

David Schmidt, 34, a history teacher by training, and his wife, Barbara, 38, an English professor at Southern Illinois University, Edwardsville, have been parishioners at St. Roch for all 10 years of their marriage. They have a son, Karl, now 9, but it was a urinary infection in their second child, Roell, that first caused concern back in June, 1975. It was the second such infection in 10 months, and the Schmidts were advised to get a special X-ray examination.

On July 28, 1975, just after Roell's third birthday, X-rays taken at St. Louis Children's Hospital disclosed that Roell's internal organs seemed normal, but that a three-centimeter calcified mass was located near her adrenal gland, on her right side. There was 99 percent likelihood the mass was a benign tumor, the doctors said, but recommended surgery as soon as possible to make certain, and to remove it.

The news started Mrs. Schmidt to worrying—and the fear and doubt that followed led her to prayer, "mainly because I just couldn't stand it anymore." Within weeks she began attending the Wednesday evening meetings of the St. Roch Parish Prayer Group, a group not unlike the hundreds that have been formed in parishes here in recent years....

After several delays caused by infections, exploratory surgery was finally performed on Sept. 9, 1975, by the team of surgical specialists at St. Louis Children's Hospital.

The results were devastating. What was thought to be a benign tumor was, in fact, 100 percent malignant cancer; moreover, cancerous cells were spread throughout the adrenal and lymph glands so extensively as to be inoperable. It was, said Dr. Vita Land, a stage III neuroblastoma. In infants under age one, such tumors sometimes dissolved on their own. But in someone of Roell's age, the doctor reported grimly, it was 95 percent fatal. There was only a 50-50 chance of prolonging Roell's life for any time at all, the doctor added, provided they began radiation and drug therapies.

Intense radiation therapy began almost immediately. So did the Schmidts' intense prayer. "Why? Because I'm a fighter," Mrs. Schmidt said firmly, "and David is, too. We began asking anyone—everyone—to pray." They solicited the prayer of David's mother's south-side prayer group, nuns in Sioux City, Jesuits at St. Louis U., the Benedictine Nuns on Morganford Rd., even Grace Methodist Church, just down the street from St. Roch Church.

Following 20 days of intense radiation, Roell began a projected 18- to 24-month series of drug therapy. The Schmidts were referred in October to another prayer resource, as well   Merton House, the residence of Father Francis MacNutt, O.P.

"Father MacNutt said he had no hesitation about praying for the healing of a child," Mrs. Schmidt related. "In fact, he said the chances for success were pretty good."

Thus, every Thursday afternoon, the Schmidts brought Roell to Merton House. Sometimes with Father MacNutt, sometimes just with his associate, Sister Mary Margaret McKenzie, V.H.M., or with others who were on hand, they would pray that God would heal Roell of cancer.

The sessions would last about 30 minutes, Mrs. Schmidt related. They would begin by Father MacNutt placing his hands on Roell's right side, approximately where the tumor was located. There was often a brief anointing with blessed oil, on the youngster's forehead and also at the site of the tumor. Then would come a period of prayer aloud. "Sometimes he would appeal for God to heal the tumor; sometimes for a change in symptoms; or for relief from the side effects of the drug therapy; sometimes he would pray in tongues." Others present who were inclined would also pray for the little girl. Then all would recite the Our Father in unison. The session would conclude with Roell leading the singing of "Everybody All Love Jesus," a nursery hymn she had learned.

At first, the Schmidts were just silent participants. "It took me three months before I was confident enough to join aloud in the prayers," Mrs. Schmidt said. She admitted, too, that the praying in tongues "seemed a little weird at first." It no longer does, she continued, "because I have received the gift of praying in tongues myself, and am comfortable with it."

Shortly after the Merton House sessions began, Father MacNutt administered to Roell the Sacrament of the Anointing of the Sick. Earlier that fall it had been given by an associate pastor of their parish. (By the time it was all over, Roell would have received some two dozen blessings with oil, although not all were the complete rite of the sacrament.)

From the beginning, the Schmidts were touched by the Merton House sessions. "Right away, the experience seemed to uplift us," David Schmidt said, and Barbara elaborated. "We felt like we had come on a pilgrimage. . . . The quality of the prayer seemed so intense and so deep. It really seemed to cut through to the heart of the matter."

In November, a small event occurred which struck the Schmidts deeply.

"One morning when I was doing the ironing," Mrs. Schmidt related, "Roell came out of her bedroom and said: 'Mommy, God says you're gonna get well.'

"'Oh,' I replied, 'I didn't know I was sick.'

"'No' she told me, sort of irritated, 'God meant that I'm gonna get well.'"

Mrs. Schmidt related the exchange that evening to her husband, who was struck by the child's use of the pronoun, "you," as if the girl was repeating exactly what she had heard.

"Neither of us dared to believe it," Mrs. Schmidt continued, "but we did take some comfort from it. And it buoyed us over a very bad time."

The times were bad, indeed. The radiation caused Roell to lose most of her hair—a common consequence—and the drug therapies were having their own severe side effect on the three-year-old: she would lose her appetite, blood counts would drop, she became feverish and caught a number of viral infections. The drugs were suspended to relieve the side effects, then the treatment cycle would be resumed.

As 1976 began, there were plans for a second exploratory surgery, to see how much good the treatments were doing, but the plans were dropped. Roell seemed to be "holding her own," the doctors related, and they recommended that the therapies be continued.

The Schmidts continued praying: Wednesday nights with the parish prayer group; Thursday afternoons at Merton House, accompanied by Roell. During Lent, they attended a "Life in the Spirit" seminar at St. Francis Xavier (College Church), and at its conclusion in April, were both "baptized in the Spirit," a kind of recommitment of belief in and witness to the Lord.

In late May, the team at Children's Hospital decided that if the drug therapies were allowed to continue, there would be permanent damage to Roell's heart, and that the time had come for surgery to both assess the effect of the treatments and to remove as much of the cancerous tumor as possible.

On June 22, the surgery was performed by Dr. Lawrence O'Neal at Children's Hospital, in which he removed the still-existing calcified mass, one-third of the adrenal gland and four lymph glands. The Schmidts and, by then, their hundreds of allies were praying intensely.

Three days later, June 25, the doctors gave the laboratory report to the Schmidts as follows:

— the tumor was found to have zero cancer cells;
— the other glands were not only free of malignancy, but were found to possess a number of ganglion,

i.e., healthy growing nerve tissue cells;

—that while the therapies may have halted the cancer cells, the medical team could not claim any credit for the appearance or growth of these healthy cells;

—such a turnaround, in patients of similar age and condition, was so very uncommon as to be remarkable.

"We were so numb from weariness and anxiety that it took a week for the news to really sink in," Mrs. Schmidt said. They promptly told Father MacNutt.

"He was thrilled, and does feel that he and the others have been God's instrument," she said.

David Schmidt, after long reflection and thought about it, attributes Roell's apparent cure this way:

"There is no doubt that prayer—especially the prayer at Merton House with Father MacNutt and Sister Mary Margaret and those with the St. Roch prayer group— have brought this about. But neither am I ready to say that the radiation and the drug therapies were unnecessary.

"We don't have medical evidence that a miracle occurred," he continued. "But neither do we have evidence that the therapies effected the cell differentiation, the cure. Who knows? Maybe someday they'll discover how this differentiation occurs.

"All I know for sure is that God cured our daughter. Whether it was through the efforts of the team at Children's Hospital or whether the malignant cells just disappeared, is a moot question."

Dr. Land calls it "the $64,000 question," but has the same assessment. "We're not sure what caused the change; all I know is that in 95 percent of the cases, the child is dead in two years."

Mrs. Schmidt adds a second blessing. "The quality of their prayer at Merton House buoyed us from week to week. Without it, our family would never have survived," she said. This is not a minor victory, she noted, inasmuch as cancer in children has an almost malevolent effect on the parents. Children's Hospital has a social worker to treat family stress among cases of children's cancer, they related.

Since June, the Schmidts have continued their weekly prayer sessions. For one thing, Roell is almost 100 percent certain to have been sterilized by the intense radiation treatments. "We pray that God, having cured her, does not allow her to perish as a result of the side effects," David Schmidt noted.

Moreover, Roell can give very encouraging witness to other cancer patients, and the Schmidts themselves feel a desire to pray for others, especially for cancer victims.

They scheduled the Aug. 23 Mass at St. Roch in order to give public thanks to God for Roell's cure, they noted, and plan to continue their prayer now a prayer of thanks.

"I've prayed for healing," David Schmidt observed, "and I've prayed in thanks and, believe me, it's much nicer to give thanks."

7. Do You Have the Gift of Healing?

Often people ask me to pray that they receive the gift of healing others. Other people write and say that someone has told them that they have the gift of healing, and now they want to know what to do.

As in most areas of Christian life, I have heard all kinds of arguments about this. Some point out that Paul in I Corinthians 12 (v. 9) talks about gifts of healing, in the plural. They reason that the one who receives the gift is clearly the person who gets healed; it is not the healer, who is simply the channel for the gift. The argument makes sense, except that the same argument could be used of all the gifts mentioned in I Corinthians 12. For example, the one who gets the benefit of the gift of inspired preaching is the listener, not the preacher. But we still say that the speaker is the one who has the gift of preaching in such a way as to touch the listener's heart.

It does seem clear that Paul is talking about special public gifts of leadership, preaching and healing (and many others) which are for the benefit of the community; it is also clear that Paul is saying that some have these gifts and not others, although everyone has been given some gift by the Spirit to build up the community.

However we understand its scriptural basis, though, I think we understand what people mean when they ask if they have the gift of healing.

And here's how I would try to answer.

The gifts, such as healing, precisely as divine gifts and not as natural endowments, are all resident in God—the Father, Son, and Holy Spirit. It is the Father, Jesus and the Spirit who heal. And they dwell within each Christian:

57

I have made your name known to them
and will continue to make it known,
so that the love with which you loved me may be in
them,
and so that I may be in them (Jn 17:26).

God is within us and his love is within us. As a result,
when we ask God to heal—and sometimes even when we
don't ask, when his very presence is in itself enough to
heal[1]—he will manifest his healing power *with* and *in* and
through us.

Every Christian, then, has the potential for healing;
and all of us, upon occasion, should pray for ourselves
and for one another when we are sick. If we all can pray
for healing, why then should anyone ask for a special gift
of healing? What sense does it make?

It makes a lot of sense if it is understood in the way
ordinary people do: that it is a fact of experience that
some people have a special gift for healing, just as some
people are better preachers than others. Everyone can
speak, but not everyone is worth coming to hear preach.

---

[1] This phenomenon occurs frequently. The following description (from a
letter) is typical:

As for my back, it is just fine, and I am confident it will not occur
again.

I had just spent four days in bed the week before the retreat. It
was a slipped disc and, as you know, it is a very painful thing; it takes
quite a while for the back to get back to normal. It was the third time
it had happened to me, but it was much more painful this time. When
I left on Friday for the retreat it was still very sore and stiff and really
bothered me when I was attending the talks.

On Saturday night my friends urged me to sit down and let you
pray for me but I was a little hesitant, thinking that there were other
people in worse shape than myself. I ended up standing beside the
last chair. When we all started to pray over one another, I forgot all
about my back but was quickly reminded when the people in back of
me started to crowd in closely and I started to move in different
directions in order to protect my back.

All of a sudden it struck me the stiffness and soreness had
disappeared, and I didn't feel a thing. I can never, never praise and
thank the Lord enough for allowing me to see his power and glory at
work in such a fantastic way.

Likewise, for whatever reason, we all know that more people seem to get healed through the ministry of certain people than others. In the days when Kathryn Kuhlman lived, a person would have to be a fool to try to hold a meeting like hers without some kind of special gift. My good friend, Barbara Shlemon, used to disclaim that she had any special gift; she would say that she was just trying to teach every Christian to pray for healing the same way she did. But after people are taught and gain some experience, that's when they really begin to appreciate more than ever the special kind of gift Barbara has.

There are parallels for the healing gift in sports and in art. All of us, unless we are severely handicapped, can play tennis or baseball. We all have that gift if we practice a little, but there are all kinds of levels in it. I can play tennis well with my middle-aged friends, but put me in a professional tournament and I am out of my class. The levels of batting excellence of baseball players are all classified in the Sunday sports pages where you can see them ranked with their batting averages, all the way from .178 up to .359. The same thing with singing. I can sing in a choir, but I don't have enough of a gift to sing solo before a crowd.

The gift of healing is a little like that; all of us can pray with our friends and relatives. But for the large public gatherings or for the more difficult cases of sickness, you need someone, as it were, who has more of this gift, more healing power, more spiritual authority, or more love.

The person with the special gift of healing is used—for whatever mysterious reason—more than others by God to heal the sick. The person with the special gift seems to have a higher *percentage* of success in praying for healing and seems to have more success in praying for the *more difficult cases* (a fact recognized by the Catholic Church in restricting the use of formal exorcism to certain prudent and holy priests).

So when persons ask us to pray that they receive the gift of healing, they should understand that what they are really asking is that Jesus multiply and increase within them a potential that every Christian has. They are asking him to increase in them a gift they already have to a certain extent, so that they can be more helpful to the sick. It's not a proud thing at all.

If this empowering indeed comes about, they won't have to go around telling people they have some kind of gift. It will soon become apparent in the extraordinary healings that take place when they simply pray in very ordinary ways for the healing of their family and friends. Word will spread, and, soon enough, people will begin to come from outside their circle of acquaintances asking for prayer and help. When people ask me how to get started with their gift of healing, it's pretty clear that it hasn't developed very far as yet; they should be more desirous of learning more, rather than of letting people know that they are available to pray. In short, we are again taling about *more or less*, rather than about having a gift or not having it.

This way of looking at the gift of healing, as a sharing *to some degree* of the life of God, is a help in other ways, too. For instance, I can understand soaking prayer better: if the degree of my life in God is less than in someone else, then it will probably take longer for the overflow of that life to penetrate the person I am praying with and to affect the diseased cells. If the degree of heat in my oven is, as it were, only 250 degrees, it will take longer for my prayer to have its effect than for someone whose fire burns at 450 degrees.

I know that I am speaking in metaphors; these are just impressions and not proofs. But this view of healing helps me and seems to account both for what I see happen and for what doesn't happen—for those who are not completely healed. My impression is that the reason why many people are not healed is not always their own lack of faith, but results rather, from a *lack of sufficient spiritual power* in the person praying for healing. After all, Jesus reprimanded the *disciples* when they could not cure the epileptic boy (Mk 9:14-29).

Consequently, I think we can say that all Christians have the ability to pray for healing, but that the effectiveness of their prayer is a question of degree. Those whom God uses in a high degree have the gift of ministering healing in the larger community: the Gift with a capital G.

There is an exception: there are a few people we meet at every workshop who cause problems when they pray for others. They have anxiety or other negative forces in them that they communicate to the person they are praying for, and this counteracts whatever good the prayer may do. I don't think we need to go into these problems in any great detail except to say that, at any given workshop, people will come and say, "I wish you would ask _____ not to pray for the rest of us. I feel very cold when he's around; whenever he's there I'm on edge." Whenever a number of people report this, someone in authority will have to protect the others from the ministration of this person, without unnecessarily hurting the person causing the uneasiness. Such problems would be avoided for the most part if people would wait to be asked before they pray— or, at least, they might ask if they can pray with someone and make it easy for them to say "no." In my experience the people causing the problems usually seem to force themselves upon others and are overly anxious to prove themselves.

GROWTH

We all have, then, the potential for healing prayer, more or less; but we can also grow in whatever gift we now have. Over the years I hope I have grown, not only through learning and experience, but in faith and in the capacity of being used by God. If we are faithful in little things, God will use us more and more for greater tasks. What we need to do is to take the first step, to pray for the sick right among us, in our families and in our communities. Maybe later, after we have grown in wisdom and power, God can use us in visiting the hospitals or leading groups in prayer for healing. People like Kathryn Kuhlman had a long apprenticeship in prayer; for years she spoke to small groups in small-town churches, before she finally developed her celebrated healing ministry. Even of Jesus it was said, "And Jesus increased in wisdom, in stature, and in favor with God and men" (Lk 5:52).

Most of us are a little afraid of all this; it seems so presumptuous to say you have a gift of healing. It's too much like saying you are holy or that you are a saint. This is a false humility, however. In Catholic Church tradition, the gift of healing (along with the others listed by Paul in I Corinthians 12) has been listed among the *gratiae gratis datae*, a Latin term which means that the gift is given for the benefit of the community, and does not necessarily sanctify the one who possesses it. In other words. I can be a sinner and still God can use me for healing, just as he might use someone who is leading a really immoral life to give a great sermon. God can truly inspire such a preacher at the time of his preaching. God gives us his healing power, because he has compassion for the sick, not because he is trying to inflate the pride of the healer. That's a humbling, sobering thought.

Frankly, there are some people who manifest some of the more extraordinary aspects of healing who do not impress me as being remarkably holy; not all of them have impressed me much as human beings. (I know we can't judge how holy people are; I'm only talking about external impressions.) One famous healer of 10 years ago, with a multimillion-dollar healing enterprise, died of alcoholism in a motel room. His friends say that when the time for a healing service came, he could rise up out of a drunken stupor, go out on the platform and speak clearly, heal many people and, then, when it was over, go back to his room and collapse.

The less said about these things, the better. But it is important to mention them briefly, if only to say that God chooses some people to heal his sick, but not to prove that the healer is holy. It's very much like his calling someone to be a priest or minister. It's a special call to help God's people, and a call to holiness, but the fact that I am a priest does not automatically make me loving or holy. I should be, and it's a greater pity when I am not. But my calling, my vocation, is one of service to God's people. It's a gift for others.

So it is with healing. If you desire to grow in a ministry of healing, do not think of growing famous. Think, rather, of growing weary in pouring out your life and energy for God's sick people. The harvest is white; the laborers are few. If you want to pray for people to be healed, you are aspiring to a wonderful ministry.

You are aspiring to be a servant.

It can help you become holy as any act of Christian service can. It doesn't presuppose that you *are* holy.

DIVERSE GIFTS

Experience also seems to indicate that some people are gifted in various areas of healing. Some people seem to have a special power to pray for certain things, but are only fair to middling in praying for other diseases.

One person, for instance, who has a remarkable and well-tested gift of healing, simply doesn't seem to have much effect in praying for cancer; when people with cancer ask for prayer, she refers them to someone else. On the other hand, a Sister I know has a particular gift in praying for cancer and has a telephone in her room where people call in from all over the world. She prays on the phone for them, apparently with great success. In his book, *Eyes to Behold Him*, Michael Gaydos speaks about his own healing of impaired eyesight and his consequent gift of being able to pray for others with the same problem.

Here and there throughout the auditorium Christians heard the word, received it, and acted upon it by taking off their glasses and removing their contact lenses. Some had their glasses back on before they left the conference, others replaced them after a day or two, some had to make appointments with their doctors for weaker prescriptions, but quite a few have never needed glasses since that evening.

...After the Charismatic Conference ended, two separate estimates of the number whose eyes God had either partially or totally healed agreed at "in excess of two hundred persons."[2]

Michael Gaydos' experience brings us to another interesting conclusion: it seems that people who have been healed of a particular ailment (e.g., alcoholism) seem to have a special gift from that point on in ministering to people with the same problem. Perhaps it's because they now have greater faith in the area in which they themselves have directly experienced God's power.

I know for myself that there are some ailments, such as deafness and loss of hearing, where others seem very successful in praying for healing, but where I have seen just a few healed through my own prayers.

On the other hand, there are ailments that are most difficult of healing, especially bone problems, where I have seen remarkable healings (usually gradual) take place. Also, when I pray for anything—except cancer—in the abdominal or chest area, I seem to have a great deal of expectancy that something will happen. Someday, perhaps, I will understand this apparent selectivity, but right now I don't. All I can say is that, humanly at least, I have a lot of confidence praying for some ailments, and much less confidence praying for others.

If your experience indicates that God isn't using you in certain areas, you might as well recognize that fact in all simplicity and ask, in prayer, if something is wrong. Or perhaps you can refer people with these ailments to someone else who seems to have better results in praying for those kinds of sicknesses.

Perhaps praying for healing parallels the specialists in the medical field. God may leave us weak in some areas and strong in others simply so we will have to rely more upon one another in community. It should not be surprising that just as there is a parceling out of ministry gifts, such as prophecy and interpretation and healing,

---

[2] From *Eyes to Behold Him* by Michael Gaydos. Copyright 1973 by Creation House, p. 68. Used with permission.

there could also be a distribution of gifts within each area of ministry as well.

Another Sister I have worked with for years has a real gift of praying for inner healing, but she says that, usually, nothing much happens when she prays for physical healing. Regardless of what we might say about why this seems to be so, she has the humility to recognize the fact and to suggest that someone else pray along with her, when she is asked to pray for physical healing.

DEGREES OF DIFFICULTY

It also seems that, just as we participate in God's healing power more or less, there are degrees of difficulty in sickness itself. It takes much more healing power to pray for a missing section of bone to grow in than to pray for a headache to disappear. Anatole France is supposed to have remarked when he visited Lourdes, that although he saw many discarded crutches decorating the grotto, he saw no artificial limbs.

We can expect then, as beginners,[3] to see more success in praying for certain kinds of ailments than others; ordinarily a deep-rooted chronic sickness will take more time, and its healing is likely to be a gradual process.

There are no exact statements I can make on which diseases seem to be the hardest to heal, but, in general, the longer a person has been sick, the more time it will take to heal. Even a severe wound, for instance, recently suffered in an auto accident, seems to heal faster than an old chronic injury.

Nor is the degree of difficulty dependent upon whether the sickness is psychosomatic or not. Some critics say that the only sickness cured by prayer is the sickness originally brought on by negative suggestion, and that our prayer just removes it by positive suggestion. My own experience indicates that some very real physical wounds caused by

---

[3] Those who are just beginning to pray for healing, though, often see extraordinary things take place. The very first person one priest I know prayed for was a blind person, who received his sight. God's gift does not depend on our experience; it is a gratuitous gift, not depending on our efforts.

accidents are changed by prayer more easily than certain deep psychological problems.

There are some ailments in which the rate of healing seems about 80 percent or so—ulcers, for example. Other sicknesses seem seldom to be healed—e.g., a paraplegic with a severed spine. I think it's important to say these things, not to diminish our confidence in prayer, but to realize that just as there are degrees of spiritual power and faith toward which we grow, there are also degrees of severity of sickness. In our ordinary lives we recognize this, but somehow in prayer groups some people lose a sense of reality.

It should not surprise us that more ulcer patients are cured in prayer meetings than paraplegics. It's not just a question of having faith. It's also a question of how much life and healing power are needed and how much of that power an individual is able to channel.[4] Some of us don't reach that instantly. I look forward to a day when I might see an amputated leg grow back or a person resurrected from the dead. But I know that the person who prays for such things must be called by God to pray in a given instance. It helps, too, to be especially gifted with faith and spiritual power. Yet, even here, God may use a weak, faltering person as an instrument for an extraordinary healing. Such is the mystery of God's love.

> Not that I have become perfect yet: I have not yet won, but I am still running, trying to capture the prize for which Christ Jesus captured me. I can assure you my brothers, I am far from thinking that I have already won. All I can say is that I forget the past and I strain ahead for what is still to come; ... (Phil 3:12-13).

SUMMARY: A QUESTION OF DEGREE

The chapters in this section have emphasized different aspects of a basic insight about the healing ministry—an

---

[4] There is also the mystery of God's will (which will be discussed in Chapter 12); healing does not depend primarily upon prayer or spiritual power. Some people will not be healed because it is not God's will for them.

insight that would solve so many problems we keep meeting in this wonderful ministry; there is a *more or less* in most of our healing prayer:

1) In *us* there is more or less of a *power or a gift* to pray for healing: for this reason wonderful things can be expected to happen when ordinary Christians pray for healing, but we seldom have anywhere near a 100 percent understanding of what we are doing when we pray, nor do we always see 100 percent results.

2) In *sickness* itself there are degrees of difficulty in healing. Some illnesses or injuries are relatively amenable to prayer, while others are very stubborn and difficult.

3) The *time* needed to pray for healing varies widely from a few seconds for something like a headache to a matter of years for something like mental retardation.

4) In *healing* there are degrees of improvement all the way from just a slight improvement to total healing.

5) There seem to be degrees in *God's own direct involvement* in the healing process. Sometimes the natural healing processes work in an ordinary way; sometimes they are accelerated by prayer, and at other times God seems to act solely through his own creative power.

This vision of the more or less and the marvelous ways God works in and through his creation should help us be more sensitive to see God's love and healing power at work in the most subtle ways. It cautions us against making absolute claims of healing or supplying proof which is not reasonably convincing. Since I have become aware of this "more or less" in healing, as distinct from "all or nothing," I can see *more evidence* of God's compassion at work than ever before.

PART TWO

PART TWO

The "Wounded Healer"

"His reputation continued to grow, and large crowds would gather to hear him and to have their sickness cured, but he would always go off to some place where he could be alone and pray." (Luke 5:15, 16)

8. The Shame and the Glory

Here I just want to say something about the pain of the human condition—of my condition in particular—trusting that it will encourage you in your struggles with the healing ministry.

THE SHAME

The problem centers on my own struggle with the thought of being considered a "faith healer." The very words cause pain, and yet, what other words are there?[1] The title "healer" is not respectable; it carries with it lower-class nonintellectual connotations that associate it with tents and evangelistic money-making schemes. A "faith healer" would be the last kind of person welcomed in a seminary or on a university campus. I am a university-type person who once taught in a seminary. Furthermore, in Catholic circles faith healing is associated with enthusiastic evangelists of an unacceptable theology and style; the Protestants, too, with whom I had ecumenical dialogue in the seminary would look down upon these faith healers as representing a type of fundamentalist Christianity that they would like to disassociate themselves from. If a "faith healer" would be met with skepticism at a Roman Catholic seminary, it is not likely

---

[1] I know that others work around the problem by calling it "divine healing" or "healing through prayer." But the problem remains. What would we call Jesus? Was he a "faith healer"? What words would we use to describe his healing activity? Again, we work around the semantic problem by calling him the "Divine Physician."

that he (or she) would be uncritically accepted at Harvard Divinity School either.

At any rate, anyone who gets involved with the healing ministry will have to live with the disrepute attached to the term "faith healer"; and if he is a Roman Catholic, he will also upon occasion meet with questions about his orthodoxy. In the early days of the charismatic renewal in the Catholic Church the healing ministry was considered even in some Catholic charismatic groups as unacceptable—part of the classical Pentecostal baggage that we were not to pick up. In 1969 I was called upon, as a theologian and as a priest, to defend the healing ministry among Catholics. For instance, I was invited to speak at Benet Lake, Wisconsin, to encourage the acceptance of the ministry of such people as Mrs. Barbara Shlemon, the Catholic nurse who had gone a lonely road since 1964 in trying to interest Catholic priests in the prayer ministry she had learned through Episcopalian friends. Even with the advent of charismatic renewal, the small Catholic prayer groups in her area were not very open to healing as an ordinary gift.

Healing was rapidly received into the Catholic charismatic renewal and most people are not even aware now of some of the opposition we initially faced. Today the wider Church is opening up more and more in a beautiful way to an understanding of prayer for healing. Yet, in the past year I have twice been publicly denounced, after talks that I have given, as a "heretic" and as a "Protestant" by priests who spoke out from the audience in question-and-answer sessions.

Then there are items such as the syndicated article that appeared nationwide featuring half a dozen people who were headlined as "aspiring to the sceptre of Kathryn Kuhlman." There, in the article, were photographs of Father Mike Scanlan and myself. If that isn't bad enough, the text describes me as the "hottest item on the Catholic charismatic circuit." Still another article appearing in the *National Catholic Reporter* describes the priests' charismatic conference at the College of Steubenville (June, 1976) and talks about my appearing in the spotlight with bare feet and a tunic looking like a rock star.

I have learned to live with and even enjoy this destruction of my old self-image as a respectable former president of the Catholic Homiletic Society, but it does make one feel like a kind of freak. And it brings with it regrettable side effects. For instance, just last week a chancery office turned down a request of the local Catholic prayer group to hold a healing service in the civic auditorium of one of our larger cities. I can well understand the fears of that chancery and their reluctance to say "yes" to a request for a healing service. I can see why they don't understand how it can be respectful and for the glory of God in his Church. I know the kind of publicity that almost always results.

But this is the price that must be paid if the healing ministry is going to return to the ordinary life of the Church. I have to let go of my desire to be considered academically respectable. Many other people who have academic credentials are going to have to get off the sidelines and have their intellectual reputations jeopardized if healing ministry is going to get into the marketplace where it belongs.

But I have to admit that I still wince when friends tell me that a prominent theologian and ecclesiastic told them, after he had skimmed my book, *Healing*, that all the theology contained therein could be compressed into a space "this big"—and here he had his thumb and forefinger about one-eighth of an inch apart. I don't like to be thought of as an intellectual lightweight; I like to see myself as a pioneer and groundbreaker in pastoral thought. But I have to be willing to let go—to be considered foolish, while trying not to be foolish. I just have to accept that in some academic circles I will be seen as reverting to a primitive world view—a reversion that they must, in conscience, attack for fear that people will be led back into superstition.[2] Even a document on

---

[2] If this fear and opposition exist in relation to healing, it is even more pronounced if the topic of exorcism or casting out of demons is brought up.

ecumenism being prepared by theologians involved in the charismatic renewal contained in an early draft a statement to the effect that large, dramatic healing services utilizing the gift of knowledge should "be resisted." I know and understand the problems connected with such services, but I really believe that a bigger problem is our desire to appear acceptable in the eyes of our scientific, rationalistic culture.

I share this desire to be accepted, to be well thought of. But my fear of losing respect can prevent me from speaking out, from acting. I think a similar fear of stepping out paralyzes the very leaders of the Church who should be showing the way—the bishops, the priests and ministers. As a result, we leave the civic auditoriums and the hordes of sick people to the ministrations of the independent evangelists whose flamboyant techniques we hold up to scorn.

We should have something better to offer the crowds of the sick; we should be pointing the way with a wise healing ministry that appeals to the multitude,[3] as well as the quiet ministry of one-to-one in the relative obscurity of our prayer groups and homes. For instance, I like to imagine that if Jesus were to return to Rome, he would soon be found in St. Peter's Square, healing the sick. A little later he would be surrounded by a crowd of ordinary people, precipitating a traffic jam, monumental even by Roman standards.

In many ways I think those of us who are Church leaders have come to follow Gamaliel rather than Peter. Gamaliel was the wise man who stood on the sidelines and urged caution, who suggested to the Sanhedrin that they wait and see if the early Christian movement would not

---

[3] The communal Anointing of the Sick is a great step in this direction. But as yet it has not afforded a large public witness of people being healed. So far this large-scale healing has either not occurred in such numbers as to be a public witness, or it has occurred but has not received public testimony. Two articles I have read in the past year describing ceremonies of communal anointing state that no healings apparently occurred, but that great spiritual blessings were received by everyone who took part.

die of its own accord, but who also warned them not to oppose it in case it should prove to be of divine origin (Acts 5:34-39). Gamaliel was surely wise and safe. But Peter was taking the risk of action; he was healing the lame man; he was incurring the anger of the spiritual leaders who were jealous because the crowds of people followed the disciples; he was disobeying the authorities who told him not to preach in the name of Jesus Christ.

In all honesty, whom do we imitate: the wise, safe, cautious Gamaliel, or Peter, who took the risk, who healed the lame man, and who preached the Resurrection?

THE GLORY

So much for the fear of criticism that is always with me—the real criticism that occasionally comes my way. But, in all honesty, the times of criticism are small in comparison to the sound of applause. Far more difficult for me to adjust to is the adulation that people who have been healed offer to the minister of healing. It's like Paul and Barnabas, after Paul had healed the cripple at Iconium, fighting off the people who wanted to make them gods and shouting, "Friends, what do you think you are doing? We are only human beings like you" (Acts 14:15).

People seem to feel that, if healings take place through your ministry, then you must be holy. But how do you react? If you say you're not holy, and mean it, they still don't believe you; they think you are just being humble. So what do you do when a woman comes into the sacristy while you are vesting for Mass and suddenly drops down and kisses your shoe? Or what do you do when people reach out as you pass by to touch a part of your coat? I certainly don't feel comfortable with all this, but there is nothing you can do, so far as I know, without making it worse. You know that people think more of you than what you really are, but you can't stop them. I remember Kathryn Kuhlman in her services saying over and over again, "It's not Kathryn Kuhlman who does it. I'm just

Joe Kuhlman's daughter from the little town of Concordia, Missouri. It's Jesus Christ who does it." As she kept repeating this, I would think to myself: Why not forget it, Kathryn, and just get on with the meeting.

One night something happened that helped me understand how to deal with all the praise. (I know the praise is real, but I feel so phony—as if people are mistaking me for someone I am not.) I was in a fair-sized meeting, praying for a number of people, one by one. I was dressed in my white Dominican robe, and as I walked along I couldn't help but notice that the people waiting were looking at me with great admiration, and it flustered me. In my own mind I prayed and asked the Lord to help me with this. I was saying, "This praise all goes to you and not me. Keep me at a distance from all this adulation." Then it was as if the Lord said, "Don't put distance between yourself and me. Just relax. What they see in you *is me*." And I saw that was true; it was good that they were seeing good! It was a help to the people and I should accept it, in a sense. Not that I wasn't human and weak with my own sins and foibles, but whatever good the people saw was truly good and was the Lord's—and also mine, in a way. I shouldn't be fighting it any more than I should fight people loving me or trusting me. They should find something lovable in me, just as I want to see what is lovable in them. And the more I see and the more the people see what is lovable, the more we give glory to God, as long as we recognize that its source is God. As soon as I saw this, something in me united and came together; I was able to continue to move down the line, praying with each person, but being content with whatever it was that anybody there was thinking. I was finally able to receive the love of the people.

It's something like the story of St. Teresa of Avila who was wondering how to be humble when she clearly had great gifts of personality, charm and intelligence. Do you beat down those gifts, as it were, and downplay them as if they are of no real importance? Well, no, she finally decided; that would be to deny the gift of God. You offer him greater praise, the more you recognize the gift and look straight at it and see how beautiful it is—but then look at the Giver, and offer thanks.

It's hard keeping a balance when some people criticize you and regard you as a religious freak, while others put you on a pedestal and regard you as a remarkably holy person.

But the balance can only be kept within yourself—where you know who God is and who you are. Neither fear of criticism nor fear of hero worship should keep you from praying for the sick.

It is only when thousands of ministers are praying for the sick that people will begin to regard the healing ministry as *ordinary*. Only then will the healer be regarded neither as an object of scorn nor as a subject for worship.

9. Having to Say No

In the last chapter I talked about how hard it is just to be yourself when you are in the healing ministry: either people think less of you than you are and you are faced with criticism, or they make too much of you and you are exalted beyond reach. Some famous names in the healing ministry have had to hide behind a barricade of secretaries and form letters. How can you just remain yourself, with no defensiveness (because of years of criticism) or no bodyguard (because of the mobs trying to reach you)?

In the past year three of my close friends in the preaching and healing ministry have more or less collapsed on the road trying to meet the needs of people for teaching and healing. How can I be sure that won't happen to me? (My schedule was as crowded as theirs.)

A large part of my sustenance has been in having a community of loving prayer support at home and on the road (I seldom work without a team). But I have also had to learn to say no, both to requests to speak and to desperate pleas from individuals. This has really been hard for me to learn. It will be for you, too, if you develop any kind of real healing ministry, for you will be swamped by requests. I have had to struggle with three seductive near-truths.

FALSE SPIRITUALITY

The first of these problems for me was a kind of false spirituality: the idea that prayer would cover every lack of human prudence. For instance, I would come into a city where I had been asked to give a talk on Friday and Saturday evenings to the prayer groups. Upon arriving at the airport Friday morning I would find that the group had, in their goodness and zeal, arranged for me to visit the hospital and pray for several desperately sick friends. Then after lunch I was to meet with the leaders of the local community to discuss various questions relating to the healing ministry. Later there was a small prayer meeting to prepare for the evening prayer meeting, and after dinner (where serious matters were again discussed) we had the prayer meeting. Following that I would stay at the home of the prayer group leader and we would prolong our discussion after the prayer meeting far into the night.

So it would go for Saturday, too, only more so, because now the phone would be ringing with desperate prayer requests from people who had heard the talk on healing the night before. These were likely to be persons needing inner healing (or even deliverance) who had not been helped in the local prayer community and believed that I could help them if only there were time for an appointment. So what to do? I would try to meet all these requests, while getting to bed at a decent time (midnight was usually the earliest we finished).

I came to realize that I was getting so exhausted that I wasn't in shape to leave on the next trip a few days later. But how could I tell people who met me at the airport that I didn't feel like going to the hospital or talking to their leaders or praying for their harder cases? If I were honest I would simply say that I would like to be left alone before my talk to rest and pray. But when I would say that, then they were likely to say, "Well, we will pray for you and God will give you new strength." If I were even more honest, I would say that it would help me to have a real change of pace—like play some tennis —instead of going to the hospital to pray. Or I would be thinking to myself, I wish I could have dinner alone, or that I knew some real friends here where we could just laugh and enjoy one another's company at dinner. I really don't want to discuss deep things at table tonight. To say these things, however, would be to blow my image of how I should act as a spiritual leader. They (and I, too, to a certain extent) believe that I should be able, except for needed rest, to engage full-time in such spiritual activities as preaching and praying and that, if, faced with a choice, I should always choose praying for a cancer patient in preference to playing tennis. How can you compare something as important as helping a sick person get better to something as frivolous as playing tennis and enjoying yourself? The only trouble is that if you are able to help sick persons be healed, pretty soon your whole life will be nothing but praying for the sick. So you can't just compare praying to tennis, and then say that praying always takes the priority. You also have to look at the balance of your entire life and to say that beyond a certain point you have, not only to rest, but to shift gears and change activities. Otherwise, you will burn out and, in the long run, end up praying for fewer people. For most of us life is a long-distance marathon, rather than a sprint, and we should pace ourselves accordingly. Perhaps all this is obvious, but there is an American tendency in me that makes me feel guilty when I am not working, and there are traces of a false spirituality still left in me that make me feel guilty about taking time out just to have fun.

Even when I am able to free myself from these binds, other people try to put me back into the role of a spiritual leader and encourage me (usually with love) to live up to their ideal. If I admit to a group that I am tired, there almost always is someone who will say, "Praise the Lord anyway," and look on me in a pitying way, as if I can never be sad or tired and be a vital Christian. Groups seem far more ready to pray for me and send me back to the fray than they are to send me to bed and send their own group home. But it's a false spirituality that leaves no room for real recreation.

Over and over I have heard people say something like, "Joe used to be so much fun to be with, but now that he's gotten involved in the prayer group, he's become *so* serious. They're always meeting and discerning over something or other." I personally was very much heartened at the International Leadership Conference in Rome (May, 1975) when I found that Father Mike Scanlan was skipping an occasional conference and jogging over to the nearby Holiday Inn to take a swim. He had simply had too many meetings over the course of a year and needed the balance; and he had the inner freedom to take that time off. On the other hand, I felt that I had spent so much money getting to Rome, that it would be a waste to miss a single talk or to lose the opportunity of meeting some of these international leaders who had so much to teach me. The truth was, of course, that I needed some time off, too, but I was bound by my notion of duty and by my fear of what others might think should they find out that I was skipping out on important talks to take a swim. I was not completely free to make the best decision; Mike had chosen the better part.[1]

---

[1] It wouldn't hurt here to mention that the schedule of most religious conferences, if followed over a long period of time, is unhealthy: long periods of sitting and listening and praying with very little break for exercise or a real time to relax at meals. It is fine for a weekend, but if you are speaking at many conferences you have to do something to break the pace. On the retreats I conduct, we usually have two hours off after lunch for siesta and exercise. The retreatants usually want more prayer and talks and suggest a shorter time off for rest, but the time is needed by the retreat team, if by no one else. In England last summer, at a four-day conference, the leaders had planned a party on the evening of the third night, but another group attacked this plan as decidedly unspiritual, since this was a rare opportunity to have a whole evening off with us to pray. (And that appealed to my sense of importance.) The sense of spiritual duty and what people "ought to do" had come into play, which led some people off to have their prayer meeting and made it hard for some of the people who went to the party to sit down and enjoy refreshments without feeling like second-class Christians. On our retreats it seems important that the retreat team be free to enjoy themselves and to take time off publicly in order to free the retreatants to lead a balanced schedule. If this is true for a retreat that lasts a few days, I think it is still more important for prayer group leaders to take the lead in changing pace and activities. Otherwise, the false spirituality, nurtured by American activism, Puritanism and Jansenism (which makes us feel vaguely sinful whenever we really enjoy ourselves) takes over the group in subtle ways.

GUILT

Spawned by this false spirituality comes a guilt that makes me ashamed to tend to my real needs and to say "no" to a request—especially a desperate, legitimate request—for prayer. Earlier this year we held a workshop on healing for leaders. One session had gone long and I thought it would be good if we could pray for one or two people after the talk, then take a break, and come back and pray for about an hour with various other individuals. So, I made the announcement, after the hour-long talk, that we would pray for two people, then have a coffee break and come back. There were several people who objected to the break, who were shocked by the thought of cutting off prayer for a while to drink coffee. They felt guilty—as if healing were God's activity and drinking coffee was worldly.

I find that I'm always struggling against this guilt that I either impose upon myself or that others would lead me to feel. The most vivid example I can remember—in fact, I will never forget it—happened several years ago on a retreat. There were several hundred people making this weekend retreat. It was impossible to pray individually with everyone who wanted help, so we tried to do as much praying as possible for the whole group. After saying a group prayer for inner healing on Saturday afternoon, I announced that, after liturgy that night, we would try to counsel and pray with as many retreatants as possible until midnight. After that announcement, just before supper, a woman came up to me and asked if I could see her after supper because she had been suffering for years from depression. I said that, no, I would be preparing for the liturgy and suggested that she try to be first in line to pray after the liturgy was over. Then she asked about making an appointment before breakfast Sunday morning. I repeated my suggestion that she take her chances, like everyone else, after liturgy, but she came back with "what are you doing at 7 o'clock tomorrow morning?" I told her the truth and said, "I'll still be resting." She returned to the attack with, "For the last 10 years I have gotten up at six every morning to prepare breakfast for my husband and children. And are you saying that you, a priest and man of God, are unwilling to get up at seven just once to talk to a woman who is thinking of killing herself?" Inside I shrunk up, feeling a cold, empty guilt, but I still said, "You can be near the head of the line tonight and I'll be sure to see you." She walked off, looking very sad; she didn't come that night.

About two weeks later, just before Christmas, I received a letter with no return address on it asking if I remembered the woman who had asked for help and been turned away. Well, she had decided to kill herself for Christmas, so she wanted to thank me for a retreat that had all the depth of an old "Gary Cooper movie." Also she noted how nicely I smiled when I said no. All this touched upon everything in me that would twist with guilt. (With the help of friends and phone calls I put her in touch with people who were able to help her over a long term.) But her story is like a parable of all the times I have had to say no; it's really hard because the person's need is usually far greater in itself than my need for rest and recreation. But because there are so many people with these needs, somewhere I have to stop, in order to survive and come back and pray another day.

The principle, of course, is that our decisions should be based upon prayer and God's will for us. As Agnes Sanford says, "Not everyone is in the bundle that we are meant to carry." But still it's hard to say no to a sick person who is asking for help and then go and lie down on your bed and rest. Yet, that's the way it really is; sometimes you have to do that. People don't even have to try to make you feel guilty; it's just their sickness pleading for help that does so. And my guilt comes into play almost automatically; my feeling that if I could take the time I ought to deny my own apparently lesser needs. But it's not just one more person; behind that person stands another with arm extended, and another and another....

Somewhere I need that inner freedom to say no if I feel God is calling me to rest or to change pace. Sometimes I envision the ultimate test; it would be on a retreat; after lunch on Saturday I have rested and have decided to play tennis for an hour before returning to speak until suppertime. As I emerge from my room, dressed for tennis with a racquet in my hand, there outside the room I see a line of 20 cripples in wheelchairs asking for prayer; they have come without appointments and are waiting. What do I do? Walk past them? Drop my racquet and start praying until the next conference, at which point I would be sapped of strength for my talk?

Yet that visualizes the real situation; every time I play tennis, the cripples are there waiting, even though I usually am in a situation where I can't see them.

But if I allow my life to be run on guilt, on being the person who always says yes, who meets the expectations that other people have about what a spiritual leader should be like, always filled with strength, always austere and taking nothing for himself, I will soon be like the man I met on my first workshop on healing. That workshop (1968) was directed by Agnes Sanford. Making the workshop was a man who was pointed out as the "Miracle Worker of _____." I thought to myself, "That must really be great; to have that kind of spiritual gift." And then I wondered to myself what it would be like if I were ever known as the "Miracle Worker of Missouri." Later I found out that he was at that workshop because he needed prayer himself, and badly; he had fallen into a deep depression and exhaustion after spending years of answering every phone call and going to hospitals late at night to pray for victims of auto accidents. When the workshop was over, this man, whom I had been envying, came up to me and said, "I would give anything to have the peace you have."

I thank him for the lesson he taught me.

COMPASSION

Hardest of all   more difficult to resist than the false spirituality and the false guilt—is for me to know (or believe) that I can heal people through prayer, and then to have to pass them by. The greater our ability to help, the more the people will come. And now we know by experience that we can help many of them. Our love increases, or should increase, as time goes by and our compassion increases as we grow older and experience some of the sufferings we never knew when we were young. So it hurts to say no to a person whom we feel we could really help if there were only time.

I know, we have heard that God will provide a way for those we cannot find time to see, but sometimes it seems as if we are the only ones available to pray. To know that we probably are able to help, that there seems to be no one else, and then to walk by; how wrenching that is.[2] We have to keep casting our cares upon the Lord and not take the burden of the world upon ourselves.

Perhaps this all seems obvious, but it is so very hard to work out in practice. I have seen many friends engaged with me in the healing work anguish so over their time that they finally had to stop all activity for months because they allowed themselves to become completely exhausted. In the beginning of learning to pray for healing our big problem is a fear that nothing will happen and we will be hurting people by leading them into false expectations. Later, as we experience how much God blesses and heals, in spite of our own pitiful weakness, it seems we have the opposite problem. It's hard to hold back and restrain ourselves, so that we don't go too far into the night praying with those who call out to us for help. Healing prayer does drain us and takes its toll.

I see these same paradoxes in the life of Jesus. I am so grateful that he was human like us: "For it is not as if we had a high priest who was incapable of feeling our weaknesses with us; but we have one who has been

---

[2] Just last month, in the midst of my giving a retreat, a lady called long distance to say that she was desperate and would kill herself that very day if I didn't help her. I called some friends in that city, who did contact her, but the next day she jumped off a building and killed herself as she had threatened if I didn't see her. All I could say to myself was that I had done what seemed best.

tempted in every way that we are, though he is without sin" (Heb 4:15). We see Jesus so moved with compassion that he heals on the Sabbath even when he knows that the synagogue leaders will turn against him. In the *New American Bible*, Luke 5:17b is translated, "The power of the Lord made him heal," almost as if he could not help reaching out when he saw someone sick and suffering.

On the other hand, we also find Jesus trying in various ways to protect himself as best he could. Often he took the sick person outside of town and, after healing him there, he would order him not to publicize it (as in Mark 1:44); I think the reason was very simple: he already had too many people following him asking for healing. When his request not to talk was ignored, he would then disappear and go off alone to pray: "His reputation continued to grow, and large crowds would gather to hear him and to have their sickness cured, but he would always go off to some place where he could be alone and pray" (Lk 5:15-16).

In Mark 1:35-38 there is a poignant description of Jesus getting up even before dawn to pray. Especially significant, he didn't even tell his disciples where he was, so that, come dawn and the rush of people, they have to go out looking for him. When Simon and the others find him, Jesus doesn't come back with them to town, but instead tells them he is going to move on to the neighboring country towns, so that he can preach in them, too. This is the diary of a hunted man and the very end of that first chapter of Mark describes Jesus' dilemma: "...Jesus could no longer go openly into any town, but had to stay outside in places where nobody lived. Even so, people from all around would come to him."

Since none of these escapes seemed to succeed, Jesus finally took his disciples away with him to gentile areas, like Tyre and Sidon, where only an occasional person would even so much as speak to him. "He left that place and set out for the territory of Tyre. There he went into a house and did not want anyone to know he was there, but he could not pass unrecognized. A woman whose little daughter had an unclean spirit heard about him straightaway and came and fell at his feet" (Mk 7:24-25).

He also tried using boats: "And he asked his disciples to have a boat ready for him because of the crowd, to keep him from being crushed" (Mk 3:9). Sometimes he used a boat to try to get away and be in a lonely place where he could be alone with his disciples, but it didn't work: "The people heard of this and, leaving the towns, went after him on foot. So as he stepped ashore, he saw a large crowd; and he took pity on them and healed their sick" (Mt 14:13-14).

Here we have a touching picture of the humanity of Jesus—he had planned different ways of getting away from the crowd, but when he saw a sick person his compassion was so touched that he changed his mind about being alone or talking with his disciples.

Improbable as it seems, I have often imagined that the human reason why Jesus walked on the water was to get to the other side of the lake without anyone being able to follow him. Yet, by a divine humor, after he made the last part of the trip in his disciple's boat, "no sooner had they stepped out of the boat than people recognized him, and started hurrying all through the countryside and brought the sick on stretchers to wherever they heard he was" (Mk 5:54-55).

Clearly, if Jesus felt it necessary to plan on how to get away from the sick, we can feel justified in laying similar plans. If you, like him, find it hard to say no, you had best, from time to time, get to some place where no one can ask you for prayer.

We need to learn to be comfortable within our human limitations. We are not God. One friend, worried about time and the number of people phoning for help, seemed to hear the Lord say: "I am willing to work within your limitations. Why aren't you?"

PART THREE

Suffering and Death

" 'If you want to' he said 'you can cure me.' Feeling sorry for him, Jesus stretched out his hand and touched him. 'Of course I want to!' he said. 'Be cured!' And the leprosy left him at once and he was cured." (Mark 1:40-42)

10. What Is God's Will in Relation to Healing?

Wherever I have spoken about suffering and sickness, I almost always experience tension: some tension in myself, knowing how hard it is to speak about these matters with balance and truth, and some tension in the audience, too—a kind of defensiveness. In Catholic groups there usually are several people who feel as if they are protecting tradition by defending sickness as a kind of blessing; it seems to them that I am preaching a kind of Christianity without a cross. On the other hand, some Pentecostals question the completeness of my faith when I talk about instances where people are not healed; they, too, feel they must defend God's honor, in that he wants everyone healed.

And yet I have spoken in private to more than one Pentecostal minister who has told me about how he has abandoned praying for healing, because he has seen the destructive results of preaching the established position that "God wants everyone healed" to his congregation and then being tongue-tied when he tried to console the wheelchair patients who were not healed at his service. Several Pentecostal ministers have also told me that their courage to conduct healing services returned when they applied the kind of teaching our teams have proposed.

In the first place, I think we must understand that sickness and suffering are a *mystery*, the great mystery of evil. Down through the centuries the Fathers of the Church have tried to give the best explanations they could (St. Augustine and St. Thomas Aquinas among them), and yet they all agree that the problem of reconciling evil in the universe with the will of an all-wise and

91

compassionate God lies beyond human understanding. So, any preaching or teaching that offers a simple answer to God's will in relation to healing and sickness, is, by reason of its easy solution, likely to be partially untrue.

Yet, it is far easier to preach in a simple way and move an audience. As Dr. Paul Tournier says:

> People who have the sort of mind that sees only one side to every question tend toward vigorous action. They succeed in everything they do because they do not stop to split hairs and have abounding confidence in their own abilities. Your successful journalist [we might add "preacher"], for instance, is inclined to simplify every problem and condense it into an arresting phrase. On the other hand, those with subtle and cultivated minds tend to get lost in a maze of fine distinctions. They always see how complicated things really are, so that their powers of persuasion are nil. That is why the world is led by those who are least suited to raising its cultural and moral standards. It is only a very few who manage to combine both tendencies, and in my view a lively Christian faith is the best precondition for the accomplishment of this miracle, because it gives both profound understanding and simplicity of heart.[1]

I think this has been the problem in the healing ministry: some recently formed Pentecostal churches and groups, frequently the victims of an anti-intellectual bias, have preached universal healing, without complete balance but with great effect, while the established churches, proud of their intellectual tradition, have preached on the subject of healing with great caution but little power.

Somewhere there must be a way of speaking which is courageous in its faith but true to reality.

Here it may help to set forth (in a simple way, I know) three positions in relation to healing and sickness:

---

[1] From *The Person Reborn* by Paul Tournier (N.Y.; Harper & Row, 1966), pp. 20-21.

1) Much contemporary theology would hold that the division between natural and supernatural is artificial. God works through the natural process, and God's healing in the world is brought through human beings using their God-given talents. New discoveries in medicine and psychology work against the very natural evils of germs, viruses and emotional problems. Talking about the devil once was a convenient way of speaking for people who did not understand the causes of their problems but who needed, in a primitive culture, a framework in which to understand the uncontrollable natural forces in the world.

Without entering into lengthy discussion on this, my own experience and understanding of scripture and a large segment of Church tradition lead me to believe that the evil that weighs upon human beings is far greater than our capacity to overcome it, and that the power of healing in Jesus Christ is way beyond our human input (which is not to deny there is a human input) when we pray for God's help.

Yet the element of truth emphasized in this position—that God is at work in the order of nature needs to be emphasized. I keep seeing people set up an opposition between what human beings do and what God does. We are all familiar with those extremists who encourage people to throw away their medicines after they have prayed for healing. Few people that I know personally would advocate such actions unless there were a real revelation on that point from God, but I often run into opposition, spoken or unspoken, when I talk to some charismatic groups about psychology in its relation to spirituality. "If you work by the Spirit, you don't need to delve into psychology" is the attitude. A number of people I have met feel that it is demeaning to God's Spirit to spend a long time in counseling to discover what needs to be prayed for; that would be relying upon "soulish" means in preference to being led by the Spirit and using the word of knowledge. Why this abhorrence of human science centers upon psychology I don't know. To the best of my

93

knowledge these persons have a high regard for astronauts, space scientists and physicians; they would never dream of asking a physician to make a "diagnosis by the Spirit" without subjecting the patient to blood tests, urinalysis, X-rays. Yet, when inner healing is brought up, there seems to be a real fear of using the human tools discovered by psychologists.

> We are so accustomed, however, to looking upon faith as being opposed to technology, that we find it difficult to imagine a reconciliation, much less a synthesis of the two. Believers are too ready to despise technology in the name of faith.[2]

This first position sees sickness as basically a natural problem that can be solved by human beings applying their intelligence and energy to eradicate it. Reliance on prayer to achieve God's "intervention" is regarded as counterproductive, leading people to depend on the "supernatural" instead of working to understand better how to conquer disease. The eradication of smallpox in our generation after a century-old struggle is a good example of what human intelligence and activity can achieve in God's plan.

2) A traditional attitude among many Catholics is that healing through prayer does take place, but that it is a more or less exceptional gift.

If anyone questions whether healing still takes place in the Church today, the traditional Catholic can always point to Lourdes and the cures attested by the Medical Bureau there. But he or she seems to have little belief that his or her own prayers for the sick will have any extraordinary effect. We were encouraged to pray for the sick, but were not encouraged to lay on hands or to have a lively belief that the sick person would get well. (A few people get defensive about this, but that was generally the truth of the matter until recently.)

---

[2] Tournier, *op. cit.*, p. 42.

On the contrary, suffering was held up as an opportunity to join with the sufferings of Christ in a redemptive way. To ask that sickness be taken away was almost like turning coward and settling for a comfortable Christianity. I know that most of my prayers in the 40's and 50's were directed to enduring sickness in a courageous way. I saw this as redemptive suffering: "Indeed, as the sufferings of Christ overflow to us, so through Christ, does our consolation overflow. When we are made to suffer, it is for your consolation and salvation" (2 Cor 1:5-6).

3) Classical Pentecostals, when they preach on healing, continually hold up God's promise of healing and intimate that God wants everyone healed. An extreme version of this view would hold that God wants everyone healed *now*. The single requirement for healing on the part of the sick person is *faith*. "If you have faith in God's promises you will be healed, because 'By his stripes you are healed.'" All the faith that a Catholic would have in the forgiveness of sins is here directed to the healing of sickness. God does not want people to be sick any more than he wants them to remain in sin.

WEAKNESSES IN THESE POSITIONS

I personally have difficulties with all these positions. The first understanding does not do justice to the magnitude of the evil we face: "For it is not against human enemies that we have to struggle, but against the sovereignties and the powers who originate the darkness in this world, the spiritual army of evil in the heavens" (Eph 6:15). The *basic* source of sickness is the primordial evil which weighs upon man and can only be lifted by a power beyond our human intelligence and activity. Over and over I have seen sick people, whom human science has been unable to help, freed or healed through prayer. This is not to deny that God is at work in our human efforts, but to say that we need a Savior, a Healer in a more direct and tangible way than most Christians have yet experienced.

The second position (that healing through prayer is extraordinary, but courageous suffering in sickness is what most Christians should expect) is deficient in its hope and it compromises on the wrong basis. It downplays God's willingness to heal and deprives many people of the healing they might have if they were led to expect that, in the *ordinary* course of events, healing takes place through prayer.

The third, the classical Pentecostal position, fails ultimately because it doesn't pass the reality test: a number of people who seem to have faith are not healed. Many thoughtful evangelists, who began with the position that God wants to heal everyone *now*, have recognized the problem and tried to answer it. Kathryn Kuhlman, for one, simply said she didn't understand why some people (including atheists) were healed and others, fully expecting healing, were not. She was honest enough to chalk it all up to mystery.[3] This classical Pentecostal position leads to much healing at their healing services; at the same time it results in some people (usually the more serious cases) being filled with guilt and inner pain when they are not healed.[4]

ATTEMPT AT A SOLUTION

Any solution will have certain weaknesses and will be intellectually unsatisfying, because evil, and that aspect of it which is sickness, is a mystery. In my previous book, *Healing*, I spoke somewhat to this question; I realize that what I said was simplified in its approach, because I wanted to emphasize what I felt was a destructive emphasis on suffering being identified as the will of God. The following points, though, I think, will be helpful to

---

[3] In my last book, *Healing*, I listed 11 reasons I had discovered that helped to account for those who were not healed.

[4] Carmen Benson in *What About Those Who Are Not Healed?* (Plainfield, N.J.; Logos, 1975), tries to answer this problem through her own painful experience and has written a fine and sensitive book.

ordinary people in seeking to understand the relationship between sickness, healing and the will of God.

IN RELATION TO SICKNESS ITSELF

This may sound obvious, but I think it is vitally important that Christians see sickness for what it is—in itself an evil and a curse. Humanly we see it that way; and when we try to see it as a blessing, we do violence to our nature—a violence which is not required by scripture.

In scripture sickness is presented as a curse. Either it is a result of the Fall—sickness being one of the traditional effects of the Original Sin of Adam—or as a punishment in some way sent by God:

> But if you do not obey the voice of Yahweh your God nor keep and observe all those commandments and statutes of his that I enjoin on you today, then all the curses that follow shall come up with you and overtake you. . . . Yahweh will strike you down with Egyptian boils, with swellings in the groin, with scurvy and the itch for which you will find no cure. Yahweh will strike you down with madness, blindness, distraction of mind, until you grope your way at noontide like a blind man groping in the dark, and your steps will lead you nowhere (Deut 28:15, 27-29).

When Christians try to see sickness as a blessing, rather than as the curse that they feel it really is—and the Bible presents it to be—then something subconsciously rebels within them. Presenting sickness as a blessing is, I believe, a pastoral response on the part of well-intentioned chaplains who want to free sick patients from any false guilt and any feeling that they are not loved by God. That is a commendable goal, but the answer is not to leave people with the impression that God directly wills the sickness for them—what friend would inflict such sickness upon me? It is rather to help them see that the sickness is part of the evil in the world that we pick up, simply because we are human and live in a fallen world. When we look at sickness, we can recognize "Some enemy has done this" (Mt 13:28), not a friend, certainly not God,

97

unless he allows it as a punishment for an individual or a group.

Most sickness is simply part of the curse which is upon our human condition, insofar as it is unredeemed; no one needs to feel individually guilty about it:

> I see this too under the sun: the race does not go to the swift, nor the battle to the strong; there is no bread for the wise, wealth for the intelligent, nor favour for the learned; all are subject to time and mischance. Man does not know his hour; like a fish caught in the treacherous net, like birds taken in the snare, so is man overtaken by misfortune suddenly falling on him (Eccl 9:11-12).

These misfortunes, including sickness, are sin of a fallen universe—not blessings sent by God

The blessing sent by God is not the sickness one sent by God to heal the sickness: his only So (The very name Jesus means Yahweh heals, saves.) This is one of the reasons why restoration of the healing ministry: so that that God, even in this life, primarily send and does not ordinarily will sickness giving power to raise us out of sick

In this way we see our deer answered. "If I am sick, why do is ordinarily not answered by this sickness for you to ac gives you," but by "God free you from this c Testament is:

He cast out th sick. This our sickne 8:16-17).

Over and ove out of evil spirits ministries represer oringing

98

suffering. I find as soon as I start to talk about praying for healing, someone usually brings up the words of Jesus in the Garden of Gethsemane, "Not my will, but thine be done," with the implication that sickness is probably God's will, and so we should accept it. This wrenches the words of Jesus out of context, for he is praying about his impending crucifixion which, as we have said, is a suffering brought upon him from without, and is not sickness. Why is this Gethsemane passage always brought up instead of the sayings of Jesus that more directly pertain to healing, such as "Cure those in it who are sick and say 'The kingdom of God is very near to you'" (Lk 10:9)? Nor do most non-Pentecostal Christians immediately think of the words of St. James,

> If one of you is ill, he should send for the elders of the church, and they must anoint him with oil in the name of the Lord and pray over him. The prayer of faith will save the sick man and the Lord will raise him up again; and if he has committed any sins, he will be forgiven. So confess your sins to one another, and pray for one another, and this will cure you" (Jas 5:14-16).

In short, when some Christians are asked to pray for healing, instead of thinking of New Testament teaching instilling hope, they pull a switch and come out with a text on suffering that emphasizes accepting it as God's will. The more I see of this the more I feel that we have been robbed of our heritage; we have learned to accept evil as good, as God's will, and have learned a hopeless rather than a hopeful response to sickness. In this we act more like Buddhists talking about karma than Christians talking about redemption.

I don't want to overdo this, because there does come a time when we must accept the approach of our death, and there are sicknesses that have not been healed which somehow we must learn to deal with and accept. For the Christian this acceptance is not a stoic one, but we should lift our experience to the level of the cross—to the level of redemptive suffering. All I am saying here is that hosts of

101

Christians have never learned that an initial response to sickness includes a belief that God might want to heal them through prayer. This belief is, by and large, simply not taught in many Christian pulpits.[6]

In the way Church teaching is interpreted, I see the distinction between suffering and sickness often blurred over. In one sentence there will be a quotation of Jesus on suffering, and the next sentence will apply this to sickness. So the confusion remains among the ordinary people who, by and large, are given no encouragement to pray for healing. They have little faith in healing prayer, because it has not been taught by their preachers or leaders. Faith in healing has been restricted to the sacraments and to particular shrines. The ability of the layman to pray for healing is ordinarily not emphasized at all.

Whether or not preachers believe in prayer for healing, I suggest that they not confuse suffering and sickness anymore in their preaching. They are not using scripture correctly when they preach on sickness by using Christ's words in Gethsemane or Paul's references to his thorn in the flesh (which do not necessarily refer to sickness at all). Why use these texts in preference to the multitude of direct references in the New Testament that deal with sickness? I think if Jesus would speak to us, he would say what he said to his disciples when they weren't able to heal the epileptic boy: "You faithless generation ... how much longer must I be with you?" (Mk 9:19).

But now a balance needs to be made. There are those who make extravagant claims (the third group) implying that God wants to heal *everyone* and *now*.

As Dr. Howard Ervin, a professor of scripture, so aptly explains in his lectures and sermons, physical sickness is not the greatest evil. *For the sake of the Kingdom* God often uses our illness for his own purposes. Sickness, as a lesser evil, can always be ordered to a higher good.

---

[6] A great change is taking place in the Catholic Church with the renewed rite for Anointing of the Sick. It is now taught as a sacrament whose principal purpose is healing.

Almost every one of us knows people who have grown magnificently as Christians and human beings because of being brought low by sickness. How often we realize that we probably wouldn't have been turned around in God's direction without sickness to help us reappraise our lives. A heart attack can help a man with an unhealthy competitive attitude toward life stop and "repent" of what he has been doing to himself (and probably his family as well).

And then there is the long Christian history of holy persons who have felt called by God to use their sickness in a redemptive way by offering their suffering bodies in union with Jesus' offering on the cross. The tradition of saints being called to this kind of redemptive suffering supports the fact that God does call some people in a special way.[7] The important thing for us to recognize is that some are called, but we are not to impose this special vocation upon *all* sick people and tell them that God has given them this cross which they should cheerfully bear. Too often, telling people that they are blessed in their sickness is a convenient way for us to escape our own lack of courage in praying for the sick.

It is important, then, for Christians to change their attitude about sickness from

seeing it generally as God's will—their share of the cross to be endured and embraced as a blessing sent by God

to

seeing that God, in general, wants to heal sickness—either through medicine or through prayer—because it is a curse upon our fallen world. Far from being a blessing, at least ordinarily, it is ultimately caused by forces of evil. Part of it will be cured in this life through the redemption won by Jesus on the cross; part will only be cured after death.

---

[7] Perhaps the most respected member of my Dominican Province in the last 20 years was Father Paschal Kelly, who was confined to a hospital bed in Minneapolis. From that bed he had as great an apostolate or greater than anyone else in our Province. He was known far and wide for his love, his cheerfulness and his wisdom.

A CHANGE IN OUR IMAGE OF GOD

The change from our seeing sickness as something willed by God to seeing health and healing as his will often has dramatic consequences in changing our attitude toward God. Again and again I have met Christians who are consciously or subconsciously afraid of God, not with the healthy fear of God we all should have, but with a deep-seated fear of letting him get too close.

As C.S. Lewis points out in *A Grief Observed*,[8] written after he saw his wife die of cancer, we are tempted to see God as a sadist if we think that he is the one willing the sickness. Lewis is saying in essence: I love my wife, and I would do anything to stop her suffering in this demeaning, wretched way. So what kind of a monster is God to let her be eaten alive by cancer? Over and over I have seen versions of this fear, of this distorted vision of God. The image Jesus presents, on the other hand, is of a loving Father who will respond by granting what we ask of him: "If you, then, who are evil, know how to give your children what is good, how much more will your Father in heaven give good things to those who ask him!" (Mt 7:11).

The fear of God that so many Christians have—the distance, too—should be a source of major pastoral concern in the Church! One of the most beautiful effects of healing in the lives of ordinary people is to open their eyes and enable them—often for the first time—to feel that God loves them. They already know it from the teaching of their churches, but it isn't the kind of heart knowledge that ultimately counts in human life.

When Paul prays that the Ephesians will know the love of Christ which is beyond all knowledge[9], he is talking about a heart knowing of Christ's love which is beyond a mere intellectual knowledge of Christ's love.

The love of God cannot be "grasped" (v. 18, using a philosophical term technical in Greek) but can be

---

[8] N.Y.; Bantam paperback, 1976.

[9] Eph 3:16-19.

"known" by a mystic's awareness of it through love. ...This awareness is something deeper than scientific knowledge, cf., I Co. 13, and is more like knowing that one is loved by the other than knowing the other that one loves, cf., Ga 4:9; even awareness of this sort, however, can never "grasp" this sort of love.[10]

What is so beautiful to me is to see a person, after he or she has received a healing, not simply rejoice in the healing itself but in a newfound sense that God really does care. This happens over and over again, and perhaps it is one reason why Jesus always found time to heal the sick when he was asked.

When we say God sends sickness or asks us to endure it, we are creating for many people an image of God they must eventually reject. What human mother or father would choose cancer for their daughter in order to tame her pride; yet, this is the kind of punishment we portray God as putting upon his people. Last year I was visiting the magnificent museum of archaeology in Mexico City, perhaps the greatest museum of its kind in the world. In it were altars, statues and a reconstruction of the ancient temple to the plumed serpent whom they propitiated by offering blood and human hearts in a massive bowl. Then, looking through the books in the gift shop, I noticed with some relief a book on the Christian art of Mexico. There it was again, this grim view, one picture after another of crucifixes in Mexican churches, dripping blood with Jesus in torment, but no picture of the Resurrected Christ. It was as if there had been a transposition from pagan God to Christian God, but no moving beyond the suffering, no sense of the triumph of the cross, no moving into Easter. It was frightening. What is presented to Christians is acquiescence in present sufferings in hope of future liberation, but no joy, no resurrection sensed at the present moment. No wonder Mardi Gras—like a pagan feast, a last fling—is the time of joy, while Good Friday,

---

[10] Footnote 1 on Eph 3:19. From *The Jerusalem Bible*, copyright © 1966 by Darton, Longman & Todd, Ltd., and Doubleday & Company, Inc. Used by permission of the publisher.

rather than Easter, is felt as the culmination of Lent.[11]

Those preachers and chaplains who try to comfort the sick by telling them to accept their illness as a blessing sent by God are giving an immediate consolation, but at what an ultimate cost! Subconsciously, the sick person must ask, "What sort of person, what kind of love, would want to see me like this? What kind of a God is this?" In a sense, we unwittingly treat God as something like a pagan deity, placated by human sacrifice.

We put the guilt on the sick person by saying, "Accept your sickness as the will of God," instead of seeing that we are failing to proclaim the good news of the Gospel because of our own fears. Let us face it, some of us don't have enough belief or courage to pray for healing.

The end result is that many of our people may believe in God, but they don't experience his love for them as individuals. They experience him as punishing and distant, and they dare not trust this kind of relationship. Do they see God as bringing sickness, or do they see sickness coming from the power that evil still has over us?

HOW DO WE SEE SICKNESS IN RELATION TO GOD?

From all that has been said, I think we can see what a person's reaction to sickness should be. It should be to see it as an inevitable part of human life because of our fallen condition; it is part of the curse that's upon us.

But God has not left us orphans. He has sent his Son with power to free us from sickness. Perhaps this will come even now as we pray. If not now, certainly eventually we will be free. If not in this life, then in the next.

---

[11] I have just been reading a letter from a missionary friend in Brazil complaining that the crowds turn out for Good Friday, but don't respond to Easter. Contemporary religious art does, of course, represent the Resurrected Christ. The crucifixion is an important, central event in the life of Christ that demands portrayal. It is only that the overwhelming symbolic attention by art in some cultures emphasizes the suffering and not the resurrected joy of Christianity.

I think it's something like being bombarded in a trench during a war. I can feel certain that God does not want war; I can believe firmly that he wants peace. But because I live in this confused world, I try to survive, to endure as best I can with spirit intact while the rockets and shells go over. I don't get involved in trying to say that God wants the war; rather, I say that an enemy has done this. I would rather be back home, out of danger, out of the filthy water. Yet, here I am, so I do my best *to endure in the midst of this evil*, until such time as it goes away. I don't have to say that the evil is God's will. In one way I accept the war, because that's the way the world is. But I also say that war is hell, and I *pray for peace!* So it is with sickness.

This dilemma is marvelously pointed up in the prayers of the Church in the Votive Mass for the Sick. Here the priest is offered two alternate prayers: one for patient endurance, the other for healing:

Father, your Son accepted our sufferings *to teach us the virtue of patience in human illness.* Hear the prayers we offer for our sick brothers and sisters. May all who suffer pain, illness or disease realize that they are *joined to Christ in his suffering for the salvation of the world,* who lives and reigns with you and the Holy Spirit, one God, for ever and ever.

All-powerful and ever-living God, the lasting health of all who believe in you, hear us as we ask your loving help for the sick; *restore their health, that they may again offer joyful thanks in your Church.* Grant this through our Lord Jesus Christ, your Son, who lives and reigns with you and the Holy Spirit, one God, for ever and ever.[12]

Notice the great difference. The priest is expected to have the discernment to make a decision: is he going to pray that the sick person be healed, or that the person will not be physically healed but will be given the inner,

---

[12] Reprinted from *The Sacramentary* (New York: Catholic Book Publishing Co., copyright 1974), pp. 916-917 (emphasis added).

spiritual strength to grow in the midst of this sickness. I propose that, ordinarily, the better prayer is that the sick person be healed. If, however, for one reason or another the person is not healed, then you do the best you can. I think this position is borne out by the Prayer over the Gifts and the Communion Prayer taken from the same Mass for the Sick. Here only one prayer is given; there is no choice for the priest to make, and the intent of both is healing, not endurance.

Prayer over The Gifts

God, our Father, your love guides every moment of our lives. Accept the prayers and gifts we offer for our sick brothers and sisters; *restore them to health* and *turn our anxiety for them into joy*. We ask this in the name of Jesus the Lord.

Prayer after Communion

God, our Father, our help in human weakness, *show* our sick brothers and sisters the *power of your loving care*. In your kindness *make them well* and *restore them* to your Church. We ask this through Christ our Lord.[13]

Here again, I think there is a parallel to war. You wish the nation were at peace; you see that God's perfect will is the human race at peace rather than at war. Yet, here you are, with circumstances beyond your control. There is war. In the midst of it you can grow, even while all the time you long and pray for peace.

Similarly, when I am sick, I pray and long for health, but it is not an anxious longing. I can also learn to grow in the midst of the sickness until such time as healing, or death, shall free me.

THE MINISTER OF HEALING

What I have learned as a minister of healing is to preach first of all about God's will to heal. I need to proclaim, to uphold, to defend that truth. Above all, I

---

[13] *Loc. cit.*

must practice it by praying for the sick.

But proclaiming this as a basic truth does not mean that I am to pray for everyone. Nor must I expect that everyone I pray for will be healed. Several of my friends, who I think listen to the Lord better than I do, have been a great help to me in this. Upon occasion, moved by pity, I have prayed for a sick person who has asked for help. At the time I noticed my friend did not join me in prayer. The person was not healed, and my friend said, "I asked Jesus if I should pray, and he said no." For whatever reason—it was not the time, or perhaps it was time to die—Jesus did not want to heal the person at the time. As ministers of healing we always need to understand our utter dependency upon God's will. It's not as if we have a power which we can exercise at our own will, our own discretion, or even according to our own compassion. It all depends upon God's perfect understanding of the situation.

Another insight I received recently (and it has deepened more and more) is that the reason some people are not healed is the minister's spiritual weakness. The epileptic boy (Mt 17:14 ff) was not healed by the disciples, and yet it was God's will that he should be healed. The discrepancy was the disciples' fault; they did not have the spiritual power to overcome a sickness of such magnitude:

"Why were we unable to drive it out?" they asked. He answered, "Because you have little faith. I tell you solemnly, if your faith were the size of a grain of mustard seed you could say to this mountain, 'Move from here to there,' and it would move; nothing would be impossible for you" (Mt 17:19-20).

The reason some sick persons are not healed has nothing to do with abstruse questions about God's will. The basic problem is in us   *we don't have enough life and spiritual power* to perform the healings that God truly wants us to perform. If I pray for someone and that person is not cured, I don't need to tell the person either that he lacks faith, or (the opposite) that he should accept

109

the sickness and endure it as God's will. Perhaps I should say that I am simply not up to it because of my own lack of spiritual power.

I don't necessarily need to feel guilty about this, since growth takes time. I need to press forward with my eyes on the goal. Usually, in talking about healing, the supernatural element is stressed, together with a down-playing of the human element: "It doesn't make any difference if___prays for you. It is God that does the healing, not any particular person." In many ways this is good.

But there truly is a human element that enters in. As we have noted, all Christians share in the ability to pray for healing. But although every Christian has this capability, there is a more or less; none of us is filled with spiritual power to the uttermost as Jesus was. I find some things relatively easy to heal (bad backs) and others much more difficult (cancer). And I have yet to meet a firsthand testimony of an amputated limb restored. If there were not a human element, there would be no more or less; there would be as many amputated limbs restored as misplaced vertebrae realigned if it were all purely God's power. To *some* are given gifts of healing.

So I must recognize that the reason many people are not healed (or are improved but not altogether healed) is not that God wills it, but it is simply a factor of my own spiritual and human weakness. I must do the best I can, humbly recognize my littleness and determine to grow more, *without straining*. I don't need to get into lengthy disquisitions about God's will; I just need to recognize that the basic reason people I pray for are not healed has little to do with God's perfect will, or to a lack of faith on the part of the sick person. If anything, it has to do with my own lack of spiritual power. I need to be more in union with Jesus, the source of that power, than I now am.

I need to minister as much life and healing as I can, recognizing that there are four degrees of healing:

a) the ideal is to remain in perfect *health*. If I were in union with Jesus, our everlasting Health,

perhaps I would never—or seldom—fall sick;
b)   to receive *healing* once I have fallen sick;
c)   to receive God's *courage, endurance,* and *comfort* if I am to suffer in the midst of sickness without being physically cured;
d)   to accept my *death* and the death process, the ultimate healing and the door to new life.

These gradations of healing are all mentioned now in the new rite for Anointing of the Sick, and healing is to take place through this sacrament on *at least one* of the four levels mentioned above.

This sacrament provides the sick person with the grace of the Holy Spirit by which the *whole man* is brought to health, trust in God is encouraged, and *strength* is given *to resist the temptations of the Evil One* and *anxiety about death.* Thus the sick person is able not only to *bear his suffering bravely,* but also to *fight against it.* A return to *physical health* may even follow the reception of this sacrament if it will be beneficial to the sick person's salvation. If necessary, the sacrament also provides the sick person with the *forgiveness of sins* and the completion of Christian Penance.[14]

Just recently, while meditating upon Acts, I received an insight I would like to share with you. It just struck me that one of the promises of Jesus was liberation, and that he was sent "to proclaim liberty to captives" (Lk 4:18). Now we know that this liberation takes place on several levels: liberation from sin, from evil spirits, and from sickness, both physical and emotional. On the larger, social scale, there is liberation from oppression and poverty. But there is also the very literal understanding of "liberty to captives," namely, freeing people from jail.

---

[14] Reprinted from *Rite of Anointing and Pastoral Care of the Sick,* Provisional Text (New York: Catholic Book Publishing Co., copyright 1974), p. 15 (emphasis added).

Luke, in writing Acts, does the same thing with "freeing convicts from jail" that he does with "resurrection from the dead" and "healing the sick." In each case, he shows Peter healing the sick, raising the dead, and being freed from prison. Then he describes incidents in Paul's life where he, too, heals the sick, raises the dead, and is freed from prison.

All of this is to show that the early Church, in the person of Peter and the other apostles, was carrying out the same work as Jesus. Paul then carried out the same activities as Peter. The gentile Church was likewise empowered to do the works (the acts) of Jesus.

Now the instructive thing about the freeing from prison episodes is that they are parallel to the healing and deliverance ministry; they show God's power at work freeing people from the forces if evil.

At first you see *extraordinary* forces at work to free the apostles from jail.

a) In the earliest jailbreak incident, the apostles as a group are arrested and then released by an *angel*, to reappear the next day preaching in the temple, much to the consternation of the Sanhedrin (Acts 5:17-21).

b) Next, Peter alone is arrested, but he escapes from prison when an *angel* appears, whereupon his chains fall off, he passes guards unnoticed, and gates open of themselves (Acts 12:1-11).

c) Next, Paul and Silas are freed by the intervention of an *earthquake* (Acts 16:25-40).

d) Then, Paul is arrested and is held in Jerusalem and Caesarea (Acts 21:27 to the end of Acts) for what was probably a total of four years (ending perhaps in 62 A.D.).

e) Finally, the solid tradition is that Peter and Paul were both imprisoned in Rome (around 67 A.D.) in the Mamertine Prison. This time they did not escape, but Peter went to his

upside-down crucifixion while Paul was be-
headed.

What must have been Peter and Paul's thoughts as
they waited in the Mamertine, strapped in their leg irons?
Peter must have thought back to the two times when an
angel came to free him. Paul would have remembered the
time when God worked through the natural processes of
an earthquake and a lengthy legal process to free him
from two previous imprisonments. Only this time it was
not to be. How can all these varied incidents be
understood on the basis of some spiritual principle that
always works, such as, "God always wants to free people
from prison."

Twice there was a direct divine intervention (the
angels), another time an astonishing natural event (the
earthquake) took place which could be seen by the eyes of
faith as no coincidence but as God causing natural force
to intervene. Then there is Paul's being freed from Roman
prisons after four years of ordinary litigation. Finally,
there came a time when—at least on the human plane—
there was no liberation, for both Peter and Paul were led
off to die.

It's that way with healing, too. At times we seem to see
a truly divine creative act—and on occasion Jesus or an
angel may even appear to the person. At other times it
seems that God moves the forces of nature to heal in an
extraordinary way, but to a skeptic you cannot prove that
it is more than coincidence. To him it is a spontaneous
remission, just as the earthquake could not be proven to
be more than a coincidence. Then, like Paul's years in
prison, there are sicknesses cured over a long period of
time by natural forces and the ordinary assistance of
medicine.

And last, there comes a time for us to welcome death
the ultimate liberator.

Which healing, which liberation, is ours when we are
sick or in prison? There is no way of telling   unless God
himself reveals it!

113

11. Suffering

This morning as I began my prayer, a pain in my body was so severe that it occupied the center of my thought. Naturally, as I began to pray I was asking for alleviation, for help. It was very hard for me to praise God. It was one of those times when I had to try to rise above it all and "praise the Lord anyway."

Clearly, pain does tend to rob us of the ability to rejoice and to praise God. The *Living Bible* translates Psalm 142 in a very realistic way: "Hear my cry, for I am very low. Rescue me from my persecutors, for they are too strong for me. Bring me out of prison so that I can thank you" (vv. 6-7). It's as if the Psalmist were saying, "How can I thank you the way I am? Free me, so that I will have something to thank you for."

The whole purpose of pain and suffering in nature is good; it's to call our attention to something that is wrong with us, so that we can do something about it and get rid of it. When I'm sick, the pain concentrates my attention on my body or emotions until I do something to get rid of the sickness. The suffering and pain are good in that they center my efforts on getting rid of the sickness which is evil and is harming me.

To call sickness itself redemptive causes difficulties— especially on the emotional level when we have to suffer through it. Some sickness is redemptive, but never on its own level. It is evil on the level of the body, and often on the level of the spirit, as well.

The whole purpose of torture, for instance, is to raise the pain level to such an extent that the person will do or say anything to be free from it. Witness what happened to the journalist, Fred Morris (son of dear Methodist friends, Rev. Hughes and Ellen Morris), when he was tortured for coming into association with Archbishop Helder Camara:

The first shocks with the electrodes went on for probably fifteen or twenty minutes. The current would increase to the point of producing muscular convulsions, and I would just be thrown to the floor. And then he would turn the current off, and if I didn't get up rapidly enough, even with my hands cuffed behind my back on the wet floor with no clothes on, he would turn on the current with light doses, like a cattle prod. As soon as I would get on my feet again, it would be the same thing: more questions, turning on the electric shock, increasing the voltage until I would be thrown to the floor again. We did that for fifteen or twenty minutes.

Then he came over and took the electrode off my breast and put it on my right ear. He sat down, and we went through the same thing, only this time the shocks were actually much more painful, going through my head. They were just indescribable. The shock, of course, would always produce some rather impressive screams.

After about fifteen or twenty minutes of that, he came and took it off my ear and put it on my penis and went back and sat down and started all over again. Not only is it extremely painful, but it triggers a nerve reaction in the legs. I was in a standing position, and when the current would get to a certain point, my legs would just simply fly up in front of me, contracting at the hips, and I would fall on my back from this height to the floor....

I think the whole first session was about an hour and a half.... By that time I was really just sort of in limbo, which is, I think, a physiological and psychological mechanism. You get to the point where it is just not real, you are really not even there anymore.[1]

To read something like this is almost unbearable; I only quote it to indicate the kind of angry, pained reaction I think we should experience when someone starts

[1] "Interview," *Sojourners* magazine, July-August, 1976, p. 22.

blithely preaching about suffering as being redemptive. Often, as in Fred's case, it becomes unbearable and leads to oblivion of the mind and spirit. Like most things in life, pain can be helpful or harmful; its purpose is to call our attention to the afflicted part so we can remove what is hurting us. A headache is not in itself naturally helpful; it is helpful in that it indicates to me that I am harming myself in some way (like worrying too much) and that I should change my life-style.

The problem, of course, comes when, like Fred Morris, we cannot change what is causing the pain. Then we have to go to another level, where we may be taught endurance or be freed of overreliance on the lower elements of life—to turn to God alone. (Fred spent the time when returned to his prison cell meditating on the Twenty-third Psalm.) Or maybe my sickness does not disappear when I pray or visit the doctor. Then I must deal with it in another way. That level of dealing with it may very well help me as a person to grow—and my sickness can be redemptive. It may even turn out that it was better for me to have suffered this sickness than to have remained in perfect health. But this is God bringing higher good out of what is in itself evil. Sickness in itself is evil at its own level (of the body or the emotions).

"Do not give up if trials come; and keep on praying" Paul says (Rom 12:12), for the natural tendency in the presence of trials is to go downhill. It is the power of the Spirit that enables us to overcome these trials.

Suffering is a part of life, pointing out to us the evil that is part of life. Some of that suffering is caused by sickness, to help us do something that will make us well. Of its very nature it occupies center stage in our attention, until we move to change. It is the body crying out for help, for pity.

As one of the effects of original sin, it will remain with me in a fallen world, until I move on to another life when "He will wipe away all tears from their eyes; there will be no more death, and no more mourning or sadness" (Rv 1:4).

Since the kingdom of God is already among us, even

now we can heal much of the suffering caused by sickness, through prayer as well as medicine.

Other sicknesses will be healed only when we stop sinning, both against ourselves and in a larger community sense. Even though Fred Morris could do nothing to stop the pain inflicted on him, the sick society that allows the torture of innocents can be changed if Christians (and others, too) begin to demand changes in our political structures.

Still, other sicknesses that I and others suffer will remain, either because we lack the spiritual power to make our prayers more effective, or because sickness, being a lesser evil in the overall plan of the kingdom of God, can have a higher, redemptive purpose in helping us to grow or to be joined with Jesus in his suffering for the human race.

But I ask those of you who are preachers not to preach about suffering—and sickness in particular—as if it were a blessing sent by God. I know that healing evangelists often preach as though God wants to heal everyone immediately and, in effect, deny that any sickness can have a redemptive aspect. That preaching can cause confusion and damage among their ailing listeners, but it is closer to the Gospel message of healing, and ultimately less harmful, than that of those preachers who speak as if endurance in sickness and not hope for healing were the Christian norm.

12. Death

Whenever we speak of healing, I think we must also think (and maybe speak) of death, because death is the *ultimate healing*.

For all of us there comes a time to be with the Lord. And it is not right for those of us in the healing ministry to speak as though God wants everyone healed, as if there were not a time to die.[1]

I suspect that many people fear death and, like Hamlet, would rather face the evils they know than go to some world outside their own experience. Consciously they may hold one thing, but deep down they fear judgment, or even harbor deep questions about what may be waiting for them at the moment of death. It was painful for me to read, for instance, Elisabeth Kubler-Ross' comment that her research into the "after-death" experiences of patients who were declared medically dead met with opposition from two groups, clergymen and scientists:

> There will be members of the clergy who will be upset by anyone who dares to do research in an area which is supposed to be taboo. Some religious representatives of a denominational church have already expressed their criticism of studies like this. One priest referred to it as "selling cheap grace."[2]

---

[1] Although, as I said in *Healing*, I think the ideal would be if people were healed even near the point of death of whatever their sickness was, and then would quietly and gently die, as softly as if they were just stepping over to the other side.

[2] From "Foreword" to *Life After Life* by Raymond A. Moody (Covington, Ga.; Mockingbird Books).

It's hard to understand why clergymen should have a hard time discussing such research, unless they fear the topic. But why?

I like Tommy Tyson's thought (given in a talk during a retreat) that someday someone might be so close to the life-giving person of Jesus that he or she would not die but simply be translated, as Enoch seems to have been, to the next life without undergoing death.[3]

Certainly, for most of us, death is the door to eternity. However much we may fear it humanly, we should anticipate it with the eyes of faith and accept it when it is at hand. So we need to pray for discernment when someone is sick to know whether we should be praying against death or not. Sometimes, we don't know how best to pray (in which case I just pray in tongues with the idea that the Spirit will pray through me for whatever is best).

Several years ago my father was 87 and failing physically. My mother was very concerned because he was not waking until three in the afternoon. He hadn't been out of the house for over six months. I thought it would be good if we could ask him to come over to Merton House where I could anoint him with the Sacrament of the Sick. We bundled him into the car and brought him over one afternoon. After the celebration of the Eucharist he stretched himself out on a couch (an original idea of his, so we could all get close enough to lay our hands on his frail body).

After the anointing, he really felt a change. He sat up and proclaimed, "I'll remember this day until I'm 110." And the next morning he was up! Along with the bodily change, he felt that his interior dispositions were changed, strengthened and sweetened (although we had always seen him as gentle and kind).

But two years later I was called to the phone during a workshop for doctors that I was giving in Minneapolis; my mother was calling to say that my father had been

---

[3] In Roman Catholic tradition, Mary, the Mother of God, was brought to heaven by Jesus, without her body having experienced corruption.

suddenly taken to the hospital. The plane that took me home did not touch down at a scheduled intermediate stop, but went straight to St. Louis, arriving 30 minutes early. When I got to the hospital and saw my father, I felt that I was not meant to pray for healing; this time I was to anoint him for strength and for everything that would prepare him for the life that comes through death. Two days later he died.

We can make a mistake, it appears, in not letting relatives or friends die when it is their time—our prayers can even hold them back. In Dr. Moody's book, *Life after Life*, relating his research on the experiences of those people declared clinically "dead," he states that "In a few instances, persons have expressed the feeling that the love or prayers of others have in effect pulled them back from death regardless of their own wishes," and quotes one person as saying:

> I was with my elderly aunt during her last illness, which was very drawn out. I helped take care of her, and all that time everyone in the family was praying for her to regain her health. She stopped breathing several times, but they brought her back. Finally, one day she looked at me and she said, "Joan, I have been over there, over to the beyond and it is beautiful over there. I want to stay, but I can't as long as you keep praying for me to stay with you. Your prayers are holding me over here. Please don't pray any more." We did all stop, and shortly after that she died.[4]

Agnes Sanford, too, reports a similar story of someone held back from death by prayer—in this case her husband, Ted. She had prayed for guidance when her husband was ill, and the Lord responded that he had three years to live. After a little over three years, he had a massive stroke, and she braced herself for his death.

> ... I did not pray for healing this time, for I knew that if Ted's life were prolonged it would be only to labor and

---

[4] *Op. cit.*, p. 8. It should be pointed out that these experiences are not the same as those *sought* after by spiritualists.

sorrow. I prayed only for whatever was best, trusting God to take him at the right time.

However, others—all his people who loved him—did not consider these matters, but prayed definitely for healing. In all my books I counsel people to ask guidance before leaping into healing prayers, but few pay any attention. Ted did make a recovery, but indeed and truly he was not himself. With help and steady upholding, he could act and talk like his old self for a time, but he could not maintain it, nor could he understand why this was so.[5]

In reading these accounts you probably have the same question that I do: If something seems not to be for the best, why does God grant it? I don't understand it either, but I think it has something to do with our freedom and a kind of authority to act that God has turned over to us. It is something like the question we have long entertained about how God could allow certain popes, bishops and priests, who seem clearly unworthy of exercising spiritual power, to have authority (which has real spiritual effects) over his people. Whole centuries of Church history seem to have been spiritually withered because of the mistakes of those who were supposed to be guiding God's people to the heights of spiritual union with Jesus Christ. Instead, they were going out to war, in armor, at the head of the papal army.

How can well-meaning people cause harm in what they pray for? What they are doing is misusing the spiritual power that has been given to them.[6] As Agnes Sanford intimates, they are not altogether without fault. They have not sought God's guidance on whether or not to pray.

Now this is especially relevant when we pray for persons we love, whose time may have come to die. Our love and our desire to have them remain with us—coupled perhaps with a certain subconscious fear of what will

---

[5] *Sealed Orders* (Plainfield, N.J.; Logos, 1972), p. 259.
[6] Just as people can speak in tongues or prophesy at inappropriate times and cause difficulties at a prayer meeting. They may have the beginnings of a genuine gift, but they misuse it.

happen to them after death—hurries us into asking God to spare them.

In reality, a true sparing would be to save them from a further time on this earth so that they might be with the Lord. I have just been reading a beautiful letter from friends of a young mother who had cancer and for whom I had prayed by her hospital bed. A short time later she died, leaving a husband, Al, and a young daughter, Lisa. Shortly after the mother died, the following incident took place:

> While Al was fixing breakfast before he and Lisa went to noon Mass one Sunday, Lisa said, "Let go of the rope, let go of the rope." Al said to her, "What are you talking about, Lisa?" She replied, "Well, that's when your Mommy gets sick and goes to the hospital and dies, and then you have to let go of the rope." "Who told you that?" Al asked. "Did Barb tell you that?" (Barb is a close friend of the family.) She just replied, "No, Jesus told me that. Did you let go of the rope, Daddy?" When Al told her that he was trying hard but hadn't done so yet, she just said, "That's all right, Daddy—I'll help you."

In God's time, though, there are possibilities of an extension being given, as it were, by God, to finish a given work or task. I have talked to one well-known charismatic leader who tells me that Jesus offered a choice: to die at a certain point or to have a three-year extension to finish a further work. I cannot vouch, of course, for the reality of the vision, but it makes sense, especially in the light of the 15-year extension granted to Hezekiah after Isaiah had told him to set his affairs in order, for he was not going to recover from his illness but was going to die. This was after Hezekiah had turned his face to the wall and prayed for a reprieve. Then the word of the Lord came to him through Isaiah, "I have heard your prayer and seen your tears. I will cure you. In three days time you shall go up to the temple of Yahweh. I will add fifteen years to your life" (Is 38:5).

Dr. Moody reports this kind of reprieve with some of

those who have recovered after being declared clinically dead:

> Several women who were mothers of young children...have told me that, while for *themselves* they would have preferred to stay where they were, they felt an obligation to try to go back and to raise their children.[7]

It's very clear that, as in all healing prayer, our first task is to seek the guidance of the Spirit. Is now the time to die? Should there be an extension? Should there be a complete healing? If we are not sure, we can simply pray and leave the outcome in the Lord's hands.

For those concerned about what to pray for because they don't receive any clear answer from their prayer for guidance, I have a good suggestion from a friend. She always prays "for healing," but not excluding death, a kind of ultimate healing. For the believer, eternal life has *already* begun; so bodily death is an event *within* eternal life. You can pray for the person's healing without necessarily praying against death. You can pray that the person be as whole as possible and ready for full union with Jesus, and leave it up to him what that might mean concretely. You can always pray for more of the life of God to enter into that person.

And this just might be *eternal* life.

In all of this the main thing is to change our attitude toward death. There is a real sense of resurrection in the preaching I hear on healing, but I do not hear the same preachers speak as often about death, in echo of Paul's triumphant cry, "Death is swallowed up in victory.

---

[7] *Op. cit.*, p. 78. It is noteworthy that all those who had "died" in this study were happy with their new condition, except those who had attempted suicide. Most were met by a being of great light and love (an angel?) who took them through a review of their lives. In most cases there was a limit that they approached but did not pass, which they assumed was the entrance into the next life.

Death, where is your victory? Death, where is your sting?" (1 Cor 15:55).

Of all the strengthening words of the liturgy, none has ever affected me more deeply than

> In him, who rose from the dead, our hope of resurrection dawned. The sadness of death gives way to the bright promise of immortality. Lord, for your faithful people life is changed, not ended.[8]

---

[8] From Preface I in the Mass for the Dead. *The Sacramentary* of the Roman Missal (New York; Catholic Book Publishing Co., 1974), p. 527. In the original Latin, the last phrase was especially poetic and succinct: *"vita mutatur, non tollitur."*

PART FOUR

Special Questions

"He called the Twelve together and gave them power and authority to cure diseases, and he sent them out to proclaim the kingdom of God and to heal." (Luke 9:1-3)

13. Sinning Against Ourselves

In *Healing* I set down the 11 reasons I had discovered why people are not healed through prayer. Since that time I have come to see more clearly that sometimes we are not healed because we must first stop "sinning" against ourselves and harming our bodies or our psychological and spiritual health. By "sinning" I don't imply that there is always moral guilt, but simply that we are often guilty of harming ourselves. We cause our own sickness, although the harm we do ourselves may not be on purpose.

I learned this, as I usually do, the hard way—by my failures. For many years, I have suffered from pain in my neck and shoulder region. Doctors have examined and X-rayed the area and found that the discs are worn down in the cervical region, and the pain comes from that, plus misalignment, presumably caused by injury (such as the time back in Army days when I was struck on the head by a batted ball when I was trying to steal home with a headfirst slide). I have had many people pray for it—including friends whom God has blessed with a great gift of healing. But nothing much has ever happened.

This is rather embarrassing, because my own greatest gift of praying for others seems to center on orthopedic problems. I have all kinds of confidence in praying for others with spinal and bone conditions. But for myself it seems different. What does it all mean?

After all these prayer attempts, it seems now that God has been wanting to teach me about two things: improving my posture, and decreasing my anxiety and learning to trust him more.

Clearly, my stooping posture contributed to the pressure on the upper spine. For many years I didn't even feel like standing straight, although my parents and friends continually called my attention to how poorly I stood. So the first step in my change took place through an inner, spiritual healing. This made me feel better about myself, so that I felt like standing tall. Up to that point every time I tried to stand erect I felt artificial, as if I were being proud. My self-image was so self-effacing I could not stand straight. So, the ultimate healing of a back problem required a spiritual healing; my posture reflected my "sin" against myself—my own poor, fearful attitude.

Similarly, anxiety created a hunching in my shoulders whenever I spoke publicly. This hunching, in turn, created physical discomfort and a twisting of the muscles and vertebrae after every lecture and sermon. It is only now, after a gradual inner healing from anxiety, that the hunching grows less. In the teaching of our Lord anxiety, too, is a kind of sin—even though it may not be intended or desired: "Can any of you, for all his worrying, add one single cubit to his span of life?" (Mt 6:27).

It is as if God has allowed the pain and the neck problem to remain in order to call attention to the deeper needs that cried for help.

As these deeper needs are being healed, the physical problem, too, can be ameliorated with the help of a chiropractor, together with a conscious attempt to change habits built up over the years and improve my posture.

There seem to be so many ailments like this. Sometimes—in fact quite often—ulcers are cured through prayer, but will that cure last if its underlying anxiety is not dealt with? More and more studies indicate that physical ailments are psychogenic, if not psychosomatic, in origin. "Psychogenic" simply means that the ailment is physical and real, all right, but it wouldn't have gotten started if something hadn't broken down on the deeper level of the human personality to let the germs or viruses or whatever win out over the body's immunity system.

For instance, there are studies now that indicate that

heart attacks are occasioned by "Type A Behavior" in which a person continually drives himself to achieve something. The Type A person is also usually working against the clock to cram as much work into his schedule as possible. This kind of person is likely to be very successful in our highly competitive culture, but what makes for business or social success is also setting him up for a heart attack at the age of 50.

If a person with a bad heart asks for prayer, healing may well take place, but his angina may also be like an early warning system by which his body is calling out for attention and indicating that the person is under too much pressure and some inner change needs to take place. It's not only that he needs more rest, but he may need a spiritual healing. Then he can learn to value himself, not just because of what he can accomplish, but because he exists and is loved by God and by friends. Typically, the Type A person has a hard time receiving love from others, and this may be the real healing that is needed; it's a heart problem all right, but what is needed is not merely the healing of the physical heart. Symbolically, it's as if the heart has been required to give, give, but has never received the consolation and rest it needs. Finally it gives out.

An excellent book on this subject is *Type A Behavior and Your Heart*[1] whose authors unabashedly state that the basic cause of heart attack is a spiritual malady which leads modern Americans to overvalue accomplishment:

No one truly enjoys having all his affairs in a state of flux. Without question all of us daydream of that time when all our pursuits are crowned with success. Realistically, most of us do look forward to the time when our car will be paid for and the mortgage retired. We also can't help looking forward almost impatiently to the time when our high-school-age children will have matriculated at a university.

---

[1] By Meyer Friedman, M. D., and Ray Rosenman, M. D. (New York: Alfred A. Knopf, Inc., 1974).

As human beings, we were not only cursed at our birth with original sin but also with the inexplicable desire to finish as fast as possible everything we begin. Unfortunately, if you are a Type A person you harbor more than just a desire to finish every project you take on. You are seized by what justly might be called a frenzy to finish everything in which you have involved yourself in as brief a period of time as possible and are willing to go to extreme lengths to do so. Thus your bent for acquisition, when tied to your "hurry sickness" leads invariably into a self-harassing state in which you chronically are confronted by dozens or even scores of processes at various stages of completion. And completion itself is the only stage that possibly can soothe or satisfy you. You habitually persist in striving to bring about a situation in which you will be able to sit back and say to yourself, "Well, everything now has been completed."

But since life itself is a series of unfinished events, your dream of achieving or reaching a state where everything will have been completed to your satisfaction is totally unrealizable. Moreover, it is particularly unrealizable in your case because as a Type A person you habitually involve yourself in or take on far more projects than anyone could finish.

It may seem to you a very sad, almost intolerable acquiescence, but part of the process of liberating yourself from the enslavement of Type A behavior is to recognize and to accept the fact that your life must be structured upon and maintained by uncompleted processes, tasks, and events. You must begin to accept your life as a melange of activities in which only some of many processes manage to get finished. And you should not cavil at the fact that perhaps the majority of your activities at any given point in time appear to be in a state of flux; you must begin to take pride in this unfinishedness. It is your reassurance that you are living. Repeat over and over to yourself this statement until finally you realize its truth: "Life is an unfinishedness."

And try to remember, when it irks you that something hasn't been finished, as rapidly as you thought it would or should be finished, it may be a hint that you are trying to run a race with death itself. After all, as a wise man once remarked, only a corpse is completely finished![2]

Many ailments that are not healed by prayer are, I think, simply the cry for a deeper reformation and healing of our personality. When, for instance, I now come down with a cold (rarely, about once a year), it is usually at a time when I have been overworking and, as it were, sinning against my body, driving it by my will. The cold, it seems to me, is like my body using the only means it has to get my attention and claim its rights. By coming down sick, it gets some rest; it won't fully combat the germs, which were there all along, until I lie down and give it the rest it needs. In a way, the cold is a good thing; it forces me to rest and get my life into balance. As I grow to be more spiritually attuned, and drive myself less by will and external circumstances, I find that I come down with colds less often. In one sense my colds and sicknesses are redemptive, but in a deeper sense they indicate that I really have been "sinning" against myself.

SICKNESS RESULTS FROM EVIL IN THE LARGER COMMUNITY

Then, too, there are sicknesses that result from sick relationships, both in the family and in the larger community. Just as the ultimate source of continued health should be living in a healthy Christian community, so a large source of sickness is outside our individual control and results from our living in sick relationships. Dr. Tom Dooley once told me that in all his work in Laos he never met a neurotic. He met psychotics, yes, but the traditional Laotian culture was based on natural rhythms and did not create the kind of neurosis generated in our American culture.

I see many painful family situations which are filled with violence, resentments, emotional repression and all

_____

[2] _Op. cit._, pp. 231-233.

kinds of harmful emotional expression. It is little wonder that emotions and bodies become chronically sick. How can we pray for *an* individual for emotional or physical healing when he or she is going right back into the destructive emotional environment that led to the sickness? That unhealthy situation may bring it back, even if it is for the moment healed through prayer.

I am reminded of an incident that occurred in a Latin American country in 1974 while I was attending a leadership conference. An Army captain came up to tell me that a general, the second in command in the country, wanted Mrs. Barbara Shlemon and me to come to his home and pray for his healing. We agreed upon a time, and a staff car came to pick us up. As we arrived at his home, we saw several soldiers marching around the grounds guarding the house.

When we were ushered into the house, much to our surprise we found a gathering of 50 people in the living room—Army officers in full uniform, men and women formally dressed—and all had gathered around a chair in the center where the general sat, surrounded by his wife and children. (It was something like a painting of a Spanish court.) After introductions, I asked the general what he would like prayer for, and he said: ulcers. Thinking to question him about the possible source of the ailment, in order to discover if there were any anxiety and, consequently, any prayer for inner healing that might be needed, I asked if we could see the general privately. We followed him into his study.

There I asked him if any anxieties or worries were weighing on him. "Yes," he said, "my enemies are trying to assassinate me."

That ended that interview, and we marched back out into the larger assembly to pray for the ulcer.

I think there are many sicknesses and ailments like the general's ulcer; the root problem requires a far bigger answer, a far greater healing. A spiritual answer to starvation in the world demands not only prayer, but that Christians be freed of their avarice and greed and be willing to share the goods that God has given them. The anger of God, as revealed in the scripture, seems especially directed against those who deprive the poor of their living and do not share what they have. "Go and sell everything you own and give the money to the poor, and you will have treasure in heaven; then come, follow me" (Mk 10:21b). Much of the evil in the world, like the starvation in Bangladesh, will not be taken away directly by God because he means for it to be dealt with by human beings—notably Christians—acting on Christian principles of love and justice. Perhaps one or another person in Bangladesh who prays will be fed by ravens, or whatever, but the larger situation, which cries out for help, will only be solved in God's plan when Christians—as nations, as churches and as individuals—are led to share what God has given them. The effect of prayer here would be to change the hearts of those Christians and nations who possess material wealth: "Sell your possessions and give alms. Get yourselves purses that do not wear out, treasure that will not fail you, in heaven where no thief can reach it and no moth destroy it" (Lk 12:33).

In short, there are some sicknesses and other human sufferings that result from the larger, communal sins of the human race, or the sins of smaller communities such as families or religious communities. These sins of hardness of heart and enmity affect even well-intentioned and saintly individuals and afflict the innocent with emotional and bodily sickness, as well as with poverty and starvation. The answer lies in *repentance*. Just as an individual needs to forgive or repent, if his sickness is caused by sin, so whole societies and communities need to repent if individuals who are affected by the sickness of society are to be healed.

For instance, people in the United States suffering from neurosis would best be healed if family relationships were more healthy, and if the values in our culture were transformed. People will continue to become neurotic, no matter how many individuals we pray for, until we "repent" in this larger sense. The overriding competitive framework of our society, for example, must be changed or heart attacks will continue to cut down 40-year-olds in

133

our Western culture. Christians seem to be just as prone to heart attacks as others, because we, too, have absorbed the harmful, unchristian competitive attitude of our society, and many Christians don't even recognize it for the destructive force that it is.

A moving example of the relation between sickness and the larger sin of lack of love was told to me by a nurse who prays often for inner healing. One day she was working in the ward where they take care of sick babies. She noticed one baby boy, much smaller than the rest, who looked as if he should have been in another section, the ward for newborn babies. In fact, he was small enough to be premature.

When she asked what was wrong with the baby, they told her that the baby's mother was a drug addict, and one night when she was out on the town she simply didn't return home. After waiting several days, the baby-sitter got tired and brought the undernourished child to the City Hospital, where he was spitting up and rejecting his formula. The nurse picked up the baby and held it for a while, and then began praying for him, asking Jesus to enter in and heal him of the loneliness and rejection and all the hurt that he had received from his mother. As she finished praying for him, the baby took his formula quietly and then fell asleep in her arms.

But as she put him back in his crib, she had the painful, horrible realization that she was giving him back—to nothing. There was no one to receive him, to love him, to give him a home. No matter how often there was healing prayer, he would go on being hurt

until there was a loving mother,
a loving home,
a loving community.

14. Large Healing Services

I have to admit that I almost always feel uncomfortable before a large healing service begins. Yet, it seems important that we have large healing services for a variety of reasons. There is a tremendous power for healing at such gatherings, especially when people have been praying and praising God for some time in preparation. To me, these healing services have been some of the greatest spiritual events I have ever attended. Although I am uncomfortable before a large healing service, when it actually takes place I am usually lifted up, way beyond my ordinary experience in praying for one or two people.

Also, there is a very practical reason for holding a large healing service: there are simply too many people needing healing to try to minister to them all, one by one. Even as I write this there are 28 people who have phoned here recently, asking for prayer for physical healing. How can I even begin to answer this need by making individual appointments? It's simply out of the question. Somehow there must be a way of praying with large numbers of people.

Then there is the public witness value of a large healing meeting. In an age when a belief in prayer for healing has largely died out, it seems to me essential that there be highly visible healing missions, so large that Church authorities cannot ignore their significance, and yet so wisely ministered that there can be no allegations that they are conducted by ignorant "holy-rollers" or moneymaking charlatans. Much as Lourdes has been a highly publicized healing shrine, conducted with impeccable honesty in its healing claims, so there need to be healing missions beautifully conducted in every city, with a high visibility to restore the healing ministry to the churches.

Yet it is clear that there are problems and questions: most critics seem to center on the question of whether we are not working on dangerous psychological ground. They fear that we are building up a mighty power of suggestion leading mostly to false or presumed healings that will fade when dawn comes. How about all those who come with high expectations and who will leave in the same sad state in which they came?

I realize these are very real problems, but I don't think they are as great as these critics make them out to be. Having participated in many large healing services (in Barquisimeto, Venezuela, in January, 1976, some 30,000 people came to a healing service held in a baseball stadium), I know firsthand about the problems. But I really think that most of them can be avoided if our preaching leads to expectant faith and we do not speak falsely or extravagantly about the faith to be healed.[1] Frankly, I think many people not directly familiar with the healing ministry don't really believe that all the healing testimonies could possibly be true, and so they tend to feel we are misleading people, albeit with good intentions. At a healing service we need enthusiastic preaching which builds up expectant faith; what we don't want is the kind of preaching where the emotions are more prominent than faith. But emotion there will always be. Preaching has to have a certain largeness, simplicity and power to reach any large crowd.[2] A constant scene in the New Testament is one of a large crowd, milling

---

[1] As described in Chapter 8, "The Faith to Be Healed," and Chapter 18, "Eleven Reasons People Are Not Healed," in my earlier book, *Healing*.

[2] I have been present at some large charismatic gatherings where priests were asked to address the multitude. Rejoicing in the unusually large number of people, the priests wanted to inject reason and balanced theology into the occasion. Their theological disquisitions, from the people's point of view (they came to celebrate), just flattened the whole occasion.

around Jesus, rejoicing and praising God. Nor are Jesus' statements encouraging people to ask for God's help nuanced or balanced with endless cautions. They are very simple, and rather startling, direct statements. He tells his followers to ask in order that they might receive, with no doubt in their hearts, but expecting that they will receive what they ask for (Cf. Mk 11:22 ff.).

I am well aware that people take the microphone and claim to be healed who are caught up in the excitement of the moment and who believe that they are healed, and the next day it turns out they were not. At times, I have misread symptoms or mistaken what the person was saying (I did this once in Nigeria to my subsequent embarrassment), but I think if we do our best to be scrupulously honest and do not exaggerate, ordinary people will have little difficulty making allowances for an occasional mistake. Regular members of prayer meetings, after all, are used to people who take the microphone from time to time, and give exaggerated testimonies; their faith isn't overly confused by such people. I think most people have a good deal of common sense; the uncomplicated way that ordinary people talk about "miracles" doesn't bother them too much. I think that they are aware that they are listening to fallible reports that are quite different from the cautious report you would get at Lourdes after a number of medical experts had examined the case.

Important as it is to get medical verification and to screen people who want to testify at meetings, there is always going to be an area of uncertainty and risk any time you let people testify at the very meeting where they have experienced a healing. But I think the immediacy of the good news is such a marvelous thing that far more is lost by suppressing these expressions of praise until weeks later when they can be medically verified.

In fact, the only people who make objections to these healing testimonies, in my experience, are the ones who are best equipped to sort out the testimonies and not be taken in: doctors and clergymen. They are professionally offended by the sloppy expressions that people use and the casual way in which they speak about miracles. They feel that they are the only ones professionally qualified to judge whether or not a miracle has taken place—and they are right. I think they simply have to remember that discussion goes on at two very different levels: one is professional and the other is the ordinary way people talk. These ordinary people aren't up to talking with professional precision, nor do most of them pretend to be. As long as the levels are not confused, no harm is done.

Yet, sometimes the professionals fear that the ordinary people are being confused by all this loose talk of miracles. I remember in Cali, Colombia, having a discussion along these same lines with a group of priests. They expressed a fear of bringing prayer for healing to the ignorant populace lest they confuse it with the spiritualistic healing many of them were involved with. One of the priests on our team, Ralph Rogawski, O.P., turned to the objector and said, "You don't know what you're talking about. We pray with the poor people in the barrios and they don't have any problems with this. It's a typical clergyman's problem. You say it's a problem the people have, but we have never seen it brought up by the people. It's your problem!"

Admittedly, there are problems in overemotional preaching that leads the sick people to experience a great letdown when they are not healed, but I think that the preacher, if he has the right attitude and balanced teaching, can lead everyone in the audience to a blessing at some level of their being, including healing. There need not be any negative effects whatsoever.

The reason I personally am uncomfortable in large healing services is that I see so many seriously sick patients who will probably need extended prayer, and there just won't be *time* to minister to them individually. Some have come from long distances—and in wheelchairs; how can we really help them?

Then there are those who need emotional healing (and perhaps even some who need deliverance) and there is hardly any way to minister to them in a large group setting. Again, there is often a need for follow-up after an initial prayer, and where will all these people find that?

If I were to spend adequate time I could perhaps pray for between five and 20 sick people in an evening. On the other hand, if I minister in some way to 1,000 people in an auditorium, perhaps 200 will be healed—or more—and many more will experience an improvement. Which is better: to pray with the individuals and see perhaps 10 healed, or to work in a more crowded and confused setting and see perhaps 200 healed?

The ideal is when the advantages of a large group setting—especially the qualities of praise and prayer— can be joined to something of the personal qualities of the one-to-one ministry. We have found several ways of doing this.

LEVEL I: Making the Healer's Prayer More Personal

My experience (and that of others, too) leads me to believe that abstract, impersonal prayers generally have little effect.[3] I can say a general prayer for healing for a group and it will have some effect, but something needs to bring it to bear upon the specific needs in the group.

One simple way of doing this (as in the ministry of T. L. Osborne, the evangelist) is to ask the people in the congregation to put one of their hands upon the ailing area of their body—provided, of course, that the area is decently accessible. Then the preacher or minister of healing can say a prayer for the entire group.

Another way is to ask all the people in the group who have a particular ailment to raise their hands if they would like prayer. ("Would anyone who has a headache or any problem in any part of your head, such as your eyes, or

---

[3] Sometimes, I think that it would be unfortunate if the ministry of healing became so accepted by the Church that a prayer were written to be said upon various public occasions (such as during the petitions of the Mass), and then it were considered that the healing ministry had been incorporated into the life of the Church. At one level I would rejoice, because such a prayer would have some effect. But still it would be nothing in comparison to the need for a more personal, intense ministry of prayer to the sick among us.

your sinuses, or your ears or any other ailment in that area, please raise your hand if you would like prayer?") Then you can say a prayer especially suited for that group of ailments. Upon occasion I have done this, praying for as many as 10 different groupings of ailments. This may all sound very simple and rather mechanical on paper, but the few times I have felt called upon to pray in this way it has seemed to personalize the prayer in a very meaningful way.

Above all, there is the "word of knowledge," made famous by Kathryn Kuhlman. Through this gift the minister of healing receives knowledge about what ailments God is in the process of healing. Kathryn would say something like, "There's a person in this section of the auditorium over here who has a back brace on. The Lord is healing you. If you take off your brace you will find your back has been healed." Sure enough, there would be a person in that area of the auditorium with a back brace, who would soon be walking up to the platform to testify to his or her healing.

The advantage in this gift is, of course, that it suddenly electrifies the crowd with the sense that Jesus is walking among them, touching one person here, another person there. At these moments the expectancy of faith is raised to its highest pitch. If she said something like "God is now touching a number of people in this auditorium who have hearing problems," whole groups of people, not just individuals, would, as it were, reach up to touch the Lord as he passed by.[4]

All this centers on something that Oral Roberts has always considered central in the healing ministry: *a point of contact.* Not only is the message of healing preached, but there comes a point when the sick person needs to reach out and touch Jesus, as it were, through some

---

[4] So important was this gift to her ministry that it was as if the singing and her preaching were merely a preparation for that time when she would have that insight into what God was to be healing that night. At times it even seemed to me that she preached overlong, waiting until that moment when the "gift of knowledge" would manifest itself in her.

gesture or object. On his television shows, for instance, he asks the viewers to touch their television sets at home while he prays for them, and he mails out bottles of oil that he has blessed that will serve as a point of contact between him and the sick person—a kind of "sacrament" or visible sign of an invisible grace.

Similarly, the "gift of knowledge" acts as a dramatic point of contact in a healing service. Some good people, not familiar with its value, express grave concerns about its being used at healing services. They fear, because there is little way to check out its authenticity. What is there to prevent someone from standing up at a prayer meeting and stating, "There are many arthritics here tonight. Claim your healing, for God wants to heal you"? In any large group there are bound to be some people who have arthritis, so how are we going to protect the people from all kinds of enthusiasts who pretend to exercise these so-called gifts?[5]

As in so many other areas, the answer to this is community. If you have worked with people for a time, you soon sort out those who have truly unusual gifts of knowledge that always prove themselves by their accuracy, from those who are guessing or who have a genuine but undeveloped, unpurified gift, which is at times exaggerated. Several people I work with in the healing ministry have these genuine gifts of knowledge; they often come up with superficially unlikely keys to illness, which ultimately prove out to be profoundly true. These gifts were first manifested and proven out over years of individual and small-group ministry. When these friends work with me and receive some insight into what ailments God is healing in the assembly, I have learned to trust them. If that assistance is suppressed and not used in the assembly, chances are the meeting will go flat.

Far from being self-serving, this gift sometimes comes on like the interior fire that the prophet Jeremiah felt searing his bones. I remember the time Mrs. Barbara

---

[5] Dr. William Nolen (*op. cit.*) had major reservations about the way this gift was exercised in Kathryn Kuhlman's services (cf. pp. 62-65).

Shlemon first experienced this knowledge gift at a public meeting (she had experienced it often in individual ministry). It was during a healing service being held in Cincinnati in a low-ceilinged church hall where the only semblance of a platform was a tiny raised area where the bingo numbers were usually read out. It was difficult for the 700 people present to see because of the numerous pillars; it was clearly going to be a difficult place to hold a healing service and to try to hold the group's attention.

As I was speaking to the group Barbara began getting vivid impressions of the various ailments that would be healed if she would simply announce that fact in faith. She fought this down twice, refusing to act like a watered-down imitation of Kathryn Kuhlman. (At least, that's the way she felt about it.) But the third time, she acted on that inspiration, and as she announced the various sicknesses being healed, a profound movement of expectant faith swept over the group.

The checks we exercise on this kind of inspiration are the same ones we have for prophecy:

1) Do we *know the person* as authentic;
2) Do their predictions *work out* in practice?
   —A proven person and a proven ministry.

It doesn't take long to check this out. The only danger is from people who operate by themselves outside the context of any possible discernment upon their ministry. But when this gift is authentic, it is a most valuable help in a large healing service.

LEVEL II: Adding Individual Ministry to the Large Healing Service

Earlier I mentioned some of the advantages of individual, one-to-one ministry. *Ordinarily* inner healing and deliverance are not ministries that can be handled at a large healing service, because of the need for time and for follow-up. *Physical* healing is the kind of healing that can best be handled at a large meeting, but even here the more severe cases usually need more time and follow-up than we can give at a large service. Happily, though, there is little negative fallout in praying for physical healing when you don't have time to pray in depth as you would like to; it's just that often nothing much happens, or that improvement gets to a certain point and no farther. Any improvement is a blessing. (In inner healing or deliverance if you get partway through and don't finish there is almost always disappointment and sometimes there is regression after a time of improvement. Especially for deliverance it is important that there be an opportunity for follow-up and, if possible, that the person be in contact with, or living in, a Christian community.)

To arrange for some kind of individual personal ministry is always a help, if it can be managed. The simplest way is for the minister of healing to be available to pray briefly for individuals after the meeting. But if there are many people, this is bound to be a drain on the speaker. If you are doing it night after night it becomes very exhausting and the amount of time you can give to each person is bound to be minimum. I almost feel that I am cheating the people who come forward with major problems: "Perhaps they will think, that because I prayed for them, they have received the kind of prayer they really need to be healed." Yet, so much blessing occurs in these imperfect circumstances, so many people are truly healed by these brief prayers, by this point of contact, that I try to pray individually with people whenever I can, provided I feel strong enough to spend the time. I can always explain to the group that this is not the ideal way to pray, that I would like to take the time to talk to each person and discover how best to pray, but, in the circumstances, we will just have to do what we can, by praying briefly for each one. This seems enough; in addition, I let them know that, if they are not healed, there will be other times and possibilities. Moreover, I can refer them to the ministers of healing in the local prayer group.

When the phenomenon of people being overcome in the Spirit occurs, that can be a great help; it's as if the Lord himself takes over and takes the time with each

143

person that we ourselves cannot give. (This, of course, depends upon its being suitably understood by the group.)[6]

Another possibility for combining individual ministry with a community healing service is to have the members of the assembly lay hands on each other while you say a general prayer, or to have them break up into small prayer groups and pray for each other. This can only be done, of course, when there is a certain level of maturity in the group. Those times when we have done it this way, with the right kind of group, the results have been phenomenal. The combination of group singing and prayer, with a sermon to prepare the way for the small group prayer, have resulted in some marvelous healings. One such combination happened fairly recently at a meeting held in a Catholic school hall in Houston. About 800 people were there, and during the small group prayer a little boy who had cerebral palsy and could only walk feebly, supported under his arms by his father, suddenly began to walk much better; he was now walking, supported only by his hand reaching up to grip his father's finger. Since then he has continued to improve. Up to this point, he had received many prayers in the prayer community, but somehow the power of God was specially present that afternoon to bring all the previous prayers up to the point of completion.

In any of this kind of large-scale ministry I try to put people in touch with some reputable minister of healing on the local scene, if it seems the sick person needs in-depth help. It doesn't take much discernment to see that some people who come forward with their physical ailments are in great need of spiritual or emotional help. In fact, these other factors may be causing the bodily problems. I can do them a real service, even if my prayers don't cure them on the spot, by putting them in touch with persons on the local scene who have the time to work with them at a deeper level.

The ideal combination, as I see it, is to have a powerful

---

[6]"Resting in the Spirit" is discussed at length in Chapter 15.

community healing service, combining the best music and the most powerful preaching possible, leading to an intense level of group prayer, and then follow that with teams of qualified people ministering to the individuals who want further prayer. On the evening of November 14, 1976, for instance, following upon a workshop of the Association of Christian Therapists, a group of people in the healing professions who also pray for their patients (nine doctors attended, with about 20 nurses, 20 priests and a number of counselors), we held a healing service at the LaSalette Shrine at Attleboro, Massachusetts. Some 2,000 people came, and 30 prayer teams (three or four from the Association comprised each team) were selected to minister individually to the people afterwards. Most of the people stayed, of course; the meeting began with celebration of the Eucharist (Votive Mass of the Sick) at 7:30 p.m., and the teams were finished praying about midnight. With four hours' time and the large number of teams of knowledgeable people we were able to minister in much more depth than usual. But getting teams of this quality, with mature Christians with an established healing ministry, is, naturally, a rare occurrence.

The following night we held a healing service at a Catholic church in Providence, Rhode Island, and here we had about 10 teams, half from the Attleboro workshop and half from the local prayer community. With some 1,500 people in attendance, this meeting (without the Eucharist) went from 6:30 p.m. until about 11:30. Because it was in a church it wasn't possible to send the teams out among the people as we had the night before (when it was held in a cafeteria), but the teams waited before the altar while the people came forward down the aisles. Again, like the night before, there was a beautiful combination of community prayer and individual ministry.

If we ever intend to help people in depth we will need, not to have fewer large healing services, but more of them; but they need to be planned in such a way as to offer individual ministry when it is needed. The most powerful healing sessions I have known—not merely as far as feelings of joy are concerned, but where the most people actually seem to have been helped—were those that combined the power and praise of a large session with something of the individual ministry that reaches out to touch each sick person where he or she needs individual help.

After all, even though Jesus was nearly overwhelmed by the crowds that sought his touch, it is not recorded that he ever had a group healing session. He touched them, one by one.

15. Resting in the Spirit

My first experience of "slaying in the Spirit" occurred in 1970. I had heard a great deal about this curious phenomenon, of how people were touched by persons who had this power and just fell over "under the power." I talked to one priest who went to a Kathryn Kuhlman meeting in Pittsburgh and was so sensitive to this power that he couldn't get near her but repeatedly fell down in the aisle as he tried to approach the platform. It sounded very strange to me. What was the purpose of it all? At first hearing, it all seemed very circus-like; moreover, it seemed to demean human dignity, and I questioned whether this was a way that God would act.

But when I saw it at a large meeting, I was struck by its effect upon the crowd: it led them to glorify God's power. Rather than demeaning people, it seemed that a real blessing, so powerful that their bodies were not able to contain it, was given to them. Then, too, I had talked to people who had experienced being slain in the Spirit, and they reported that they had felt as light as a feather when they fell; and that during the period when they lay on the floor, they had experienced great peace and the sense of God's presence. That inclined me to be favorable; it was worthwhile if the main effect was a real interior blessing and not merely some external flashy sign that some evangelists used to attract the crowd.

So, when I got up in front of a large crowd and an evangelist noted for having this unusual power approached to pray for me, I welcomed the opportunity. If Jesus wanted to bless me in some deep interior way, I didn't want to resist; I want to receive any real blessing there is. (Also, as a true Dominican I wanted to understand for myself what this was, in case I was ever called upon to explain it.)

I stood there, determined not to fight it—whatever it was. A "catcher" stood behind me, while several thousand people watched. I felt the gentle pressure of the evangelist's hand on my forehead. I was faced with a decision; if I didn't take a step backward, the pressure would push me off balance, and I would fall. But I thought to myself: I don't want to resist in any way if this is of God.

So I fell—all 6 ft. 4 in. The crowd made a noise—a combination of surprise and delight at seeing a priest in a Roman collar succumb to the power of God.

Then I quickly scrambled to my feet, not sure that I hadn't just been pushed. Again the evangelist prayed; again I felt the pressure on my forehead which I did not resist. Once more I fell.

It was confusing. Others, I knew, had experienced something good. But if I had only my own experience to go on, I would have judged that nothing in particular had happened to me. Moreover, I wondered if it wasn't simply my being pushed off balance. I didn't know what to make of it all.

IN MY OWN MINISTRY

In time, though, and almost imperceptibly, I began to see it happen in front of me as I prayed for others. At first it only happened when I was helping someone else pray. For instance, I remember (in 1971 I think it was) praying with Tommy Tyson for an older man who was seated on a chair. This man acted as though he had fallen asleep and almost fell off the chair. I remember being surprised that Tommy was not surprised, or worried that the man had suffered a heart attack.

But then, about a year later, some few people I was praying for would seem to experience this in a very mild way. Since I usually did not pray for people who were standing, but only when they were sitting, all I had to do to stop any swooning was to stop praying.

I do remember one notable exception, though. It was on a retreat in 1971 for priests and seminarians. The group had put up considerable resistance to the then-new charismatic retreat, but we had gotten to the point of praying as a group. About 100 priests and seminarians, with three Visitation Sisters who were on the retreat team, were crowded into the prayer room. Most were sitting on the floor, a few were standing, and there were only a few chairs. When we asked if anyone felt ready to ask for the baptism of the Spirit, one seminarian volunteered. We put one of the chairs in the center, and Father Joe Lange and I prayed for him. Afterwards there was a hush, and it seemed that much silent prayer was going on. Then another seminarian asked for prayer, so I asked the first one if he would move so we could use the chair again. To our surprise he said, "I can't move." Rather than call attention to this strange occurrence, we simply moved out a second chair. All during the subsequent prayers the first seminarian remained sitting there. After about an hour, he asked a friend to adjust his glasses, for they were slipping down over his nose. It was certainly unusual; he looked all right, he was able to talk, but he couldn't otherwise move, so we tried not to call any attention to his plight.

When it was finally time for the meeting to break up, more than two hours later, he still remained behind, immobile. So our team gathered around him to find out what was happening. As we prayed he finally said, "I seem to keep hearing, 'without me you can do nothing.' During my whole life I have always controlled everything. Now I'm going to turn it over to God." And with that he began to move, and five minutes later he left the room. At the time it seemed like a rather dramatic lesson, somewhat like the symbolic actions the prophets performed to make a point in an unforgettable way. Only here it seemed that God was making the point. Only later did I realize that it was, in part, the phenomenon of "slaying in the Spirit."

Those times, though, when I noticed that something like this was happening, I would stop praying before anything external happened. I saw no point in leading people to look for extraordinary happenings that would cause reasonable on-lookers to wonder whether something overemotional wasn't going on. If these people blacked out, I figured, it would inhibit anything in the spiritual order that God might want to accomplish. After all, what I saw in those evangelists' meetings where this took place were people falling over and getting immediately to their feet. The rapidity with which all this took place, the carnival atmosphere, hardly led to the impression that anything deep was going on in people's spirits.

But then several people I prayed for experienced this and proceeded to rest for a considerable time. Afterwards, they told me of some really deep spiritual experience they had while in this state. I began to wonder if this state related in any way to the "ecstasy" mentioned in the lives of the mystics of the Church, in which the intensity of a spiritual experience was so great that the senses and the body were temporarily incapacitated, as in St. Paul's celebrated experience:

> I know a man in Christ who, fourteen years ago, was caught up—whether still in the body or out of the body. I do not know; God knows—right into the third heaven. I do know, however, that this same person—whether in the body or out of the body, I do not know; God knows was caught up into paradise and heard things which must not and cannot be put into human language (2 Cor 12:2-4).

TRADITION OF THE CATHOLIC CHURCH

All of this put me in mind of some things I had read about in the lives of saints and others who had written of their spiritual experiences down through the ages of the Church. St. Teresa of Avila, for instance, had written of experiences where the body fell away, as it were, because of the intensity of what it was experiencing. In her autobiography, for instance, she writes:

While seeking God in this way, the soul becomes conscious that it is fainting almost completely away, in a kind of swoon, with an exceeding great and sweet delight. It gradually ceases to breathe and all its bodily strength begins to fail it: it cannot even move its hands without great pain; its eyes involuntarily close, or, if they remain open, they can hardly see.... He can apprehend nothing with the senses, which only hinder his soul's joy and thus harm rather than help him. It is futile for him to attempt to speak: his mind cannot form a single word, nor, if it could, would he have the strength to pronounce it. For in this condition all outward strength vanishes, while the strength of the soul increases so that it may the better have the fruition of its bliss. The outward joy experienced is great and most clearly recognized.

This prayer, for however long it may last, does no harm; at least it has never done any to me, nor do I ever remember feeling any ill effects after the Lord has granted me this favour, however unwell I may have been: indeed, I am generally much the better for it. What harm can possibly be done by so great a blessing? The outward effects are so noteworthy that there can be no doubt some great thing has taken place: we experience a loss of strength but the experience is one of such delight that afterwards our strength grows greater.[1]

Teresa's experience resulted, of course, from her great union with God—she was an extraordinary saint; but I also remembered what had happened to ordinary people through the ministry of John Tauler, a German Dominican preacher of the 14th century.

I had read his story when I was a novice in Winona, Minnesota, back in 1950, and it always stayed with me. John was a famous preacher in Cologne, and one day he was talking in the sacristy to a layman who had been taking notes on his sermons. When John pressed him to say what he thought of John's preaching, the layman was

---

[1] *The Life of Teresa of Jesus*, trans. by E. Allison Peers. (Garden City, N.Y.; Image Books, 1960). Pp. 177-178.

very reluctant to speak; but finally he was pressed to say that he felt John was like the Pharisees who operated more out of the pride of intellect than by the light of the Spirit. John was, naturally, cut to the heart. After an interior struggle, he offered to take the unusual action (especially for that era) of submitting himself to the layman's direction. This man told John to stop preaching and to pray and study for a time. When John did this, his Dominican brothers thought he was becoming unbalanced and ridiculed him. Then, one day, as he was praying in the midst of great suffering,

> . . . he heard with his bodily ears a voice that said: "Stand fast in thy peace, and trust in God. And remember that when He was on earth in His human nature, when He cured men of bodily sickness, He also made them well in their souls." The moment these words were spoken, he lost all sense and reason, and knew not whether he was carried away nor how. But when he came to his senses again, he found a great change had taken place in him. All his interior and his outward faculties were conscious of a new strength; and he was gifted with clear perceptions of matters that had before been very strange and alien to him.[2]

The layman's response to this event was remarkable:

> I say to thee that now for the very first time thou hast been touched by the Most High. And this thou must know: as formerly the letter had somewhat killed thee, so now shall the same make thee alive again. For now thy teaching comes from God the Holy Ghost, whereas before it was from the flesh. Now thou hast the light of the Holy Ghost, received from the grace of God, and thou hast the holy Scriptures in thee. Therefore hast thou now a great advantage, and in the future far more than formerly thou shalt understand the Scriptures, for thou knowest full

---

[2] *The Sermons and Conferences of John Tauler*, trans. by Very Rev. Walter Elliott, C.S.P. (Private printing of 500 copies by Apostolic Mission House, Washington, DC; 1910), p. 30.

well that the Scriptures in many places seem to contradict themselves. But now that in the light of the Holy Ghost thou hast received divine grace to possess the Holy Scripture in thyself, so wilt thou understand that all Scripture has the same meaning and is never self-contradictory.[3]

In short, it seems that John Tauler, a revered spiritual author of my Dominican Order, was "slain in the Spirit." But what is important is not the bodily manifestation, but what went on within his spirit: he was

1) touched by God in an experiential way for the first time, and
2) he received the Gift of Understanding.

In time the layman gave him permission to begin preaching again—some two years after he had gone into seclusion and silence. At his first sermon he started weeping so profusely that he couldn't preach, for which he was further ridiculed by his Dominican brothers. But then he tried again. This time he preached with such effect that—

When this sermon was over, the Master[4] went and offered Mass.... But fully forty men staid behind in the churchyard lying as it were in a swoon. Now the man who had previously given counsel to the Master, when he learned of this, told the Master of it, and when the Mass was over he led him to the churchyard that he might see these people and consider what ailed them. But while Mass was being said they had risen up and gone away, all but twelve, who still lay there. Then the Master said to the man: "Dear son, what thinkest thou we should do with these men?" Then the man went from one to another of them and touched them. But they moved very little, and lay there almost as if they were dead. This was a very

---

[3] *Ibid.*, p. 31.
[4] In this account John Tauler is referred to as the Master since he was a Master of Sacred Theology, a title given in the Dominican Order.

strange thing to the Master, for he had never seen the like before.... Then the man said: "These men are still alive, and I beg thee to request the Sisters' leave to have them carried under shelter, lest by exposure to the night air and by lying on the cold earth, they should catch cold." And so the Master had them carried to a warm place. Then the Sisters said, "Dear sir, here is one of our sisters to whom the same thing has happened, and who lies in bed as if she were dead."[5]

Later they went to the Master's room where the layman spoke:

Didst thou ever see the like of this in thy whole life? Thou now seest plainly what wonders God will do by one who is a fit instrument of his work. Dear sir, I foresee that this sermon will move many people, and they will discuss it one with another. If it be thy will, I would advise that thou leave these weak children awhile in peace, for they must have a long time to deal with this discourse.[6]

From my remembrance of having read this account from the traditional spiritual literature of the Roman Catholic tradition, I was helped not to be surprised by the novelty of it all, but to see that such extraordinary phenomena could happen to ordinary people (Tauler's Life referred to them as "these weak children"); that the basic purpose was to give them some *interior* blessing (in this case, to absorb the meaning of the sermon); that an external publicity purpose was not altogether improper (the people would "discuss it one with another"); that it is regarded as a great benefit to ministry ("Thou now seest plainly what wonders God will do"); that these phenomena do not seem to occur until Tauler, or whoever the minister of God is, becomes filled with a certain measure of God's power for ministry; that a person "slain in the Spirit" could expect to spend some time in this condition and that its duration varied.

---

[5] *Ibid.*, pp. 39-40.
[6] *Ibid.*, p. 40.

All of these considerations, in the back of my mind, prepared me not to turn away from "slaying in the Spirit" if it were a blessing being offered by God As I say, I only saw this happen in my ministry from time to time, and it was usually not even noticed by those standing by, because we prayed for people sitting down.

IN PROTESTANT TRADITION

I was also aware, through reading Ronald Knox's *Enthusiasm*[7] that many of the famous Protestant revivals had been characterized by people "swooning." In the preaching of John Wesley, the founder of Methodism, this phenomenon was common:

While Molther and Hutton were trying to convince Wesley that the only way to attain true conversion was to wait for it in perfect stillness, he was preaching at Bristol, to people who cried as in the agonies of death, who were struck to the ground and lay there groaning, who were released (so it seemed) with a visible struggle then and there from the power of the devil.[8]

Because of the swooning phenomenon and the cries and trembling that often went with it, Wesley was widely criticized.[9] Since the news media picked up these outlandish phenomena first, and reported them, Wesley's work was subject to question from more staid churchmen.

Shortly afterwards the same falling to the ground attended the preaching of Wesley's disciple, George Whitefield, in the U.S.A. (around the year 1740):

"Some were struck pale as death, others were wringing their hands, others lying on the ground, others sinking into the arms of their friends." His position on the matter is curious. He had preached many times in Bristol without

---

[7] A Galaxy Book. N.Y.; Oxford University Press, 1961. Quotations reprinted with permission of the estate of the late Ronald Knox.
[8] *Op. cit.*, p. 472.
[9] *Op. cit.*, p. 505.

producing any remarkable symptoms, and when they began to emerge, he was disposed to register a protest to Wesley: "Honoured Sir, I cannot think it right in you to give so much encouragement to these convulsions which people have been thrown into under your ministry. Were I to do so, how many would cry out every night?" But when he discussed the matter with Wesley in person, he was severely reprimanded by the logic of facts. The very next day, when he, Whitefield, was preaching, "four persons sank down close to him, almost in the same moment."[10]

Another evangelist friend of Wesley's, John Berridge (whom Ronald Knox describes as admirably level-headed) preached with such effect that "Great numbers, feeling the arrows of conviction, fell to the ground, some of whom seemed dead, and others in the agony of death, the violence of their bodily convulsions exceeding all description."[11]

Noteworthy, it seems to me, is that so much of this swooning occasioned by 18th-century preaching was accompanied by convulsions, rather than by the peace which ordinarily accompanies the resting in the Spirit that I have seen. I would agree with what Wesley himself believed was the cause of the more distressing symptoms: 1) that, since the sermons had to do with conversion, there would naturally be outcries and sobbing; 2) that grace was mingled with emotional disturbances, such as hysteria; and 3) that some people were afflicted by demonic forces and needed to be set free.[12]

I have to admit that I don't feel comfortable with the violent types of phenomena described in early Methodist revivals, but I am more inclined to accept Wesley's understanding of it   especially since the fruits of it were good—than to pass it all off as hysteria. Observe the following accompaniments to Wesley's preaching, about which he was happy:

---

[10] *Op. cit.*, p. 526.

[11] *Op. cit.*, p. 527.

[12] *Op. cit.*, p. 535.

At Limerick in 1762, "Many more were brought to the birth. All were in floods of tears, cried, prayed, roared aloud, all of them lying on the ground."[13]

At Newcastle in 1772, "An eminent backslider came into my mind, and I broke off abruptly...'Is James Watson here? If he be, shew thy power.' Down dropped James Watson like a stone."[14]

At Coleford in 1784, "When I began to pray, the flame broke out. Many cried aloud, many sank to the ground, many trembled exceedingly."[15]

IN THE UNITED STATES

The fainting away that accompanied George Whitefield's preaching (described earlier) was one of the phenomena accompanying the "Great Awakening" of the American frontier. A further wave of revivalism broke over the U. S. at the beginning of the 19th century, and we read about the Shakers,

...trembling, weeping and swooning away, till every appearance of life was gone, and the extremities of the body assumed the coldness of a corpse. At one meeting not less than a thousand persons fell to the ground apparently without sense or motion.... Towards the close of this commotion, viz. about the year 1803, convulsions became prevalent.[16]

Men and women fell in such numbers that it became impossible for the multitude to move about without trampling them, and they were hurried to the meeting house. At no time was the floor less than half covered.[17]

Another great revival broke out before the Civil War in the late 1850's, and perhaps the most famous preacher

---

[13] Wesley's *Journal*, 28/7/1762.

[14] *Op. cit.*, 5/6/1772.

[15] *Op. cit.*, 8/9/1784.

[16] Marguerite F. Melcher, *The Shaker Adventure* (Princeton, N.J.; Princeton Univ. Press, 1941), p. 14.

[17] Knox, *op. cit.*, p. 62.

connected with it was Charles G. Finney, who was, at the time, a level-headed Presbyterian, concerned about undue emotionalism and conversions that were not rooted in deep conviction. The first time that people were overcome by his preaching was one afternoon in Utica, New York, when some 400 people fell off their chairs onto the floor after he had been speaking about 15 minutes.[18] Many years later he reflected on such manifestations:

> In every age of the Church, cases have occurred in which persons have had such clear manifestations of Divine truth as to prostrate their physical strength entirely. This appears to have been the case with Daniel. He fainted and was unable to stand. Saul of Tarsus seems to have been overwhelmed and prostrated under the blaze of Divine glory that surrounded him. I have met with many cases where the physical powers were entirely prostrated by a clear apprehension of the infinitely great and weighty truths of religion.
>
> With respect to these cases I remark:...
>
> That they are not cases of that objectionable excitement of which I spoke in my former letter. For in these cases, the intelligence does not appear to be stultified and confused, but to be full of light. The mind seems not to be conscious of any unusual excitement of its own sensibility; but, on the contrary, seems to itself to be calm, and its state seems peculiar only because truth is seen with unusual clearness. Manifestly there is no such effervescence of the sensibility as produces tears, or any of the usual manifestations of an excited imagination, or deeply moved feelings. There is not that gush of feeling which distracts the thoughts; but the mind sees truth, unveiled, and in such relations as really to take away all bodily strength, while the mind looks in upon the unveiled glories of the Godhead. The veil seems to be removed from the mind, and the truth is seen much as we must suppose it to be when the spirit is disembodied. No wonder this should overpower the body.
>
> Now such cases have often stumbled those who have

---

[18] *Autobiography.*

witnessed them and yet, so far as I have had opportunity to inquire into their subsequent history, I have been persuaded that, in general, these were sound cases of conversion.[19]

In more recent times "being slain in the Spirit" has characterized the preaching and healing services of Kathryn Kuhlman, Kenneth Hagin, Mr. and Mrs. Charles Hunter, and many others—mostly independent evangelists. The Hunters, in a little book called *Since Jesus Passed By*,[20] describe at some length how "falling under the power" (as they term it) first happened in their meetings and then increased in their ministry of praying for people—to be converted, healed and delivered.

We do not pretend to understand this supernatural manifestation of God's power, but have accepted it as a current demonstration of God's power. The first time it ever happened to us was shocking! While we were praying for a woman at the altar, there came the feeling that she "wasn't there any more." We opened our eyes, and sure enough, she "wasn't there any more." She had been touched by the power of God and was lying on the floor.

A short time later, this recurred. Again, only once during a service! Then a few months later it happened again. Each time it came as a complete surprise to us. Neither of us felt any special anointing... nothing....

Then came February 27, 1973, El Paso, Texas. The power of God fell in a mighty way. The power could almost be heard crackling as a Southern Baptist Church had its own day of Pentecost. Somewhere around 100 people fell under the power of God. Probably the most surprised of all the people there were the Hunters. We had never seen anything like this happen in our ministry and certainly couldn't understand it, but we discovered an interesting fact. GOD OFTEN DOES A SUPERNATU-

---

[19] Reprinted by permission from *Revival Fire* by Charles Finney, published by Bethany Fellowship, Inc., Minneapolis, MN 55438. pp. 34-35.

[20] Reprinted from *Since Jesus Passed By* (Van Nuys, CA; Time-Light Books, 1973).

RAL WORK IN HEALING, DELIVERING OR
CLEANSING WHILE A PERSON IS UNDER THE
POWER.[21]

The Hunters quote many letters describing the deep
spiritual benefits of people who have been under the
power and describe such unusual events as some 200 out
of 1,700 people falling, with no one touching them at
Northern Colorado University at Greeley, Colorado.
This happened when the people were offering a clap-
offering to the Lord (instead of applauding the Hunters).
"Suddenly, all over the ballroom people had fallen out
under the power of God. Some were laughing, some were
praising, and speaking in tongues, some lay still, and
when we left at 11:30, there were still a few on the floor
under the power of God in this way. *No human had
touched them.*"[22]

On another occasion as many as a thousand people
fell,[23] and on still another, in Wichita, Kansas, some 50
pastors, including several priests, and five Catholic sisters
all fell gently backwards after prayer.[24] Yet, in the early
days of their ministry, they wondered why so few miracles
happened. "We had prayed for probably 10,000 people
and only on rare occasions were people healed, maybe 10
or 20, and then we were honestly surprised."[25] It was only
later, after they had learned to rely more upon the Spirit
that more healings took place. Then, when the phenomenon of "falling under the power" began to take
place, still more healings seemed to take place. So the
Hunters understand this phenomenon as being a sign of
the intensity of God's power being present.

IN MY OWN MINISTRY

My own experience parallels that of the Hunters in

---

[21] *Op. cit.,* pp. 16-17.
[22] *Op. cit.,* p. 123.
[23] *Op. cit.,* p. 23.
[24] *Op. cit.,* p. 139.
[25] *Op. cit.,* p. 23.

some ways. It was about three years ago, when I was praying for a few people, one by one, after Mass on Pentecost Sunday, that I noticed that most of the people (there were about 15) seemed to be a little groggy after prayer. They were standing as I prayed, and several fell. Then, following a very powerful prayer for increased help in ministry by a group of friends in Clearwater, Florida, a team member and I were ministering together after a talk by Derek Prince in a Presbyterian church in Washington, D.C., at a large ecumenical meeting. This time everyone we prayed for, except one, was overcome in the Spirit. Since that time it has been happening regularly—not always, but on occasion. So I had to try to see what it was all about in order to know whether we should encourage it or ignore it until it happened or, perhaps, even to discourage its happening.

Since then it has also been happening in the ministry of other priests and ministers, notably at two parishes in Massachusetts.

•

WHAT IS IT?

Talking to many people who have experienced it, as well as observing what was happening at our meetings, I came to some understanding of its meaning. So far as I can see, it is the power of the Spirit so filling a person with a heightened inner awareness that the body's energy fades away until it cannot stand. In the 10th chapter of Acts, the author speaks about Peter falling into a trance; in the description of Gethsemane we read about the soldiers falling backwards when Jesus spoke to them; and Paul fell to the ground during his conversion experience. All these experiences seem to have been similar to the phenomenon that some call "being slain by the Spirit."

In his essay on slaying in the Spirit Father George Maloney, S.J., states that the descriptions in scripture of Daniel (Dn 10:9) and Paul (Acts 9:4) falling to the ground are not the same as what happens today in slaying in the Spirit, because they were experiencing ecstasies directly from God and "Ecstasy is not the same as one falling into

161

a faint through the mediation of another other than Jesus Christ."[26] Admittedly, some slaying in the Spirit appears to be primarily a bodily phenomenon, a power phenomenon, yet many people do experience something like ecstasy from which the bodily phenomenon follows.

And often this is without mediation of anyone's laying on hands. Last month during the celebration of the Eucharist, at a meeting of just 100 people invovled in the healing professions, five persons were overcome in the Spirit during the prayers of the Mass, without anything further being added, and with no one touching them.

More recently still a pastor wrote to me:

> During the Saturday liturgy at Mt. Augustine, Staten Island (Dec. 19, 1976) I was distributing Holy Communion. About 40 persons received from me. Two of them were overcome in the Spirit when I placed the host on their tongues. I was quite surprised, but I didn't think too much about it at the time.
>
> The next day a young man spoke to me about it; he said that all his life he had grave doubts about the presence of Jesus in the host. He was overwhelmed with faith in the Eucharist when he saw the two people fall.
>
> I had never had this experience before, nor have I heard of it before. It was a really unique experience for me.

Because most people who experience this phenomenon report that they are more alive than ever interiorly, I prefer not to speak of it as being "slain in the Spirit," which only refers to something external, a body falling to the ground. It's quite the opposite of being "slain"; it's

---

[26] "How to Understand and Evaluate the Charismatics' Newest Experience: "Slaying in the Spirit,'" *Crux*, Nov. 1, 1976. (Single copy 35¢ with self-addressed, stamped envelope from *Crux*, 75 Champlain Street, Albany, N.Y. 12204.) Father Maloney's article is cautionary and deals with many of the dangers involved with slaying in the Spirit.

more like too much life for the body to bear. So I'm for getting rid of the word "slain" which connotes violence.

TERMINOLOGY

With these questions in mind, Father Michael Scanlan (president of the College of Steubenville) and I discussed whether there wasn't something better to call this phenomenon. We came to the conclusion that we would refer to it as being "overcome by the Spirit" in order to "rest in the Spirit." These terms more adequately describe what actually happens.

In the history of the Church a term which bears some similarities is "rapt in ecstasy"—ecstasy comes from Greek words which refer to the spirit "standing outside the body."[27] Then others, like Charles and Frances Hunter, use the term "falling under the power," which does certainly describe what happens. In the summer of 1975, when this phenomenon began to occur in a Catholic gathering in England, the wise and witty Monsignor John O'Connor suggested that the British would understand and accept the phenomenon if we referred to it with the understatement, "A touch of dormition."[28]

There is a wonderful description of resting in the spirit, using those very words, by Saint Birgitta of Norway:

"Oh sweetest God, strange it is what Thou dost to me! For Thou dost put my body to sleep, and my soul Thou awakenest to see and hear and feel the things of the spirit. When it pleaseth Thee, Thou dost send my body to sleep,

[27] In ecstasy the emphasis is on an intense union with God in which the senses and body fade away, as it were. The terms "being overcome by the Spirit" or "being slain in the Spirit" refer more to the bodily phenomenon of falling which may or may not accompany an intense experience of union with God. In ecstasy some degree of mystical union with God is ordinarily presupposed; in "being overcome by the Spirit," a degree of union with God is not necessarily present.

[28] Dormition had just the right overtones of "rest" and tradition as in "The Dormition of the Blessed Virgin," while the word "touch" emphasized its gentleness.

not with bodily sleep, but with rest of the spirit, and my soul Thou dost awaken as though from a trance to see and hear and feel with the powers of the spirit."[29]

THE PURPOSES OF RESTING IN THE SPIRIT

When someone truly receives a touch from God, it is always helpful (providing it truly is from God). This interior touch varies all the way from a person's merely experiencing peace and joy—which are beneficial in themselves—to a very deep and direct contact with God, sometimes through vision, sometimes through a locution (word). After talking to many people and reading their letters after their experiences of being overcome by the Spirit, there are several real advantages when people seek the interior benefits and not the externals.

1) Experiencing the presence of God. Many people who experience resting in the Lord experience not just the rest and peace, but the Lord himself in some way. As one Sister describes it:

How I wish I could find words to express my profound gratitude for the deep joy and abiding peace that have invaded my being during these past few weeks . . . for all that has become since then, and now each day as I continue to grow in the Spirit. One of the most beautiful gifts that have come to me is to know that Jesus is Lord and Savior, and that He really cares . . . that He loves me. I have always known this intellectually, and we even "teach" it to our students. But to know this in truth and in fact, to feel it deep inside the marrow of my bones, has made all the difference in the world—especially my world, my life. . . .

It is so vitally important because it truly is a matter of life or death. I know this is true for me. And I've been praising Jesus all my waking hours and sleeping ones too. To be able to come to a deeper sense of awareness and to

[29] As quoted in *Saint Catherine of Siena* by Johannes Jorgenson, translated from the Danish by Ingeborg Lund, Longmans, Green and Co., London, New York and Toronto, 1938, p. 15.

know for sure that Jesus is for real . . . that He loves me beyond my wildest dreams and imagination. This is a miracle and more; it is life, His Life, His Love.

I want to shout out to the whole world, "Come, see, and taste and know that the Lord is God, and Good, and all loving and kind."

These words do not come from a high school girl but a 40-year-old Sister with many years of teaching experience.

Sometimes when we pray for healing, the healing does not take place, and yet there is a real gift of God's presence as described in the following letter:

On June 11, 1975, when you so kindly offered personal ministry, you laid hands on me and prayed for healing of arthritis, hiatal hernia and sinusitis. The awareness of the presence of Jesus and the joy were so intense that I was overpowered in the Spirit. That awareness stays with me, although I have not received the healing physically. The really important thing is that I know Jesus better each day.

At times, this encounter is a conversion experience. For instance, during the International Charismatic Conference in Rome, May, 1975, I prayed for the healing of a woman who had been in an auto accident more than 10 years before, and who was still suffering its effects throughout her body. After praying 10 minutes, the pain and other effects all left her, and she was rejoicing (she was not overcome in the Spirit). Later in the day, however, I saw her again, and she looked downcast; when I asked her if anything had gone wrong, she said that all the pain was back, worse than ever. So I began to pray again and asked the Lord, if he wished, to deal with this problem by the power of the Spirit. She did fall; she rested for about five minutes, then stood up again, radiant. She had seen a great light, and said that she heard the Lord tell her, "Surrender yourself to me and I will heal you." So she surrendered, and then was healed.

2) This brings us to the second purpose: *to facilitate healing when there is no time* to really talk and pray as you would like to, especially when there are crowds of people. Then, if a person is overcome in the Spirit, the Lord may heal or deliver the person in a quicker way than ordinarily. Sometimes, as in the above example, when I don't know what's wrong and don't have time to ask, the Lord will simply deal with it himself. Last summer, for instance, a priest who had suffered from mental depression for years and was under a psychiatrist's care, asked if I could pray with him. Since I was speaking at a large conference, and prayer for inner healing usually takes an hour or so, I told him I couldn't manage the time. But later while I was just praying briefly for him in tongues, he was overcome in the Spirit and rested for some two hours. During that time, as he described it later, the Lord came and took him through his whole life, explained the meaning of some of his painful experiences, and healed them. Some things that the priest had thought were important turned out to be relatively unimportant, while Jesus showed him nearly forgotten incidents that had left a deeper imprint. One thing the Lord told him that has remained with me: "Do you realize that the people *you* forgive, I will forgive too? You can truly loose your enemies." At any rate, the priest was healed through a one-minute prayer (on my part) that turned out better than if I had tried to counsel and pray with him myself for two hours. I should emphasize here, though, that this kind of thing only occasionally happens; usually we have to pray the ordinary prayer which takes time. Even when a person is overcome by the Spirit, it doesn't necessarily mean that anything deep has happened. Often we need to go through an extended prayer, just as we ordinarily would.

3) A third reason I have found why resting in the Spirit is helpful is when a *special power* of God is needed in difficult cases. This is especially true in deliverance when evil spirits are present. It makes it much easier, because the power of God is so strong that anything evil has a hard time surviving in its presence; it is driven off by the excess

of God's goodness and then doesn't have to be cast out directly. Or, if casting out is needed, the evil spirits surrender more easily. This also is true of healing; this special power seems to make healing easier, more seems to take place than ordinarily, and it happens more quickly. Often it's as if the Lord himself takes over and gives the counseling and healing and gifts needed by the person:

> I asked for the spirit of anxiety to be taken from me and the infilling of his peace. As you prayed over me a great power forced me back. I was trying to stay on my feet; as the force became less I could see a bright light and I was as if caught up in it. I've never seen anything so bright. I remember singing joyfully as I witnessed this brightness.
>
> The next morning I awoke in a spirit of peace I have never known, and I could smell the scent of roses. . . . I was in that state of peace quite a few days.

Another Sister writes that after she was overcome in the Spirit—

> The Lord showed me my fellow religious and gave me the grace of forgiveness and a genuine love for each of them. He showed me that the Sisters I am to live with this year will be drawn closer to him, and the principal, whom I had such a fear of, is his child and before the year is up she will be made aware of that reality. He took away all my fears.
>
> He then became like a little child and showed me the classroom I will be teaching in, and, as we entered the room, a beautiful calm and peace pervaded the room. I asked him how I am to maintain this calm attitude, and Jesus pointed behind me and when I turned I saw Mary standing at the teacher's desk. She told me that she is going to help me love these children with her love. With her I am going to give birth to them. Then Mary interjected, "You have now been truly consecrated as a spouse of Jesus. You are now all his."

Following this the Lord led her to further reconciliations with her religious community and with her mother and family. Mary then suggested that she spend more time reading scripture in order to learn more about Jesus, and encouraged her to spend the rest of the evening praying at the altar until her friends came to drive her home.

I find that this kind of experience occurs fairly commonly when people are resting in the Spirit. In no way does it show that a person is holy, nor do we necessarily have to accept each revelation as genuine. It is only by their fruits that we shall know them; but, over and over, people report that they experience a peace, a joy a greater love of God. Upon occasion they also receive healing (both physical and inner) and conversion. As St. Teresa of Avila observes,

> And let none of you imagine that, because a Sister has had such experience, she is any better than the rest; the Lord leads each of us as He sees we have need. Such experiences, if we use them aright, prepare us to be better servants of God; but sometimes it is the weakest whom God leads by this road; and so there is no ground here either for approval or condemnation. We must base our judgments on the virtues.[30]

In fact, this is what I have discovered: that helping people rest in the Spirit is a real *ministry gift*. I use it for ministry, while it seems that most evangelists use it after ministry as a simple demonstration of God's power.

OTHER OBSERVATIONS

As for the time element: I have seen it last anywhere from a few seconds to six hours. If it lasts some little time, there is more chance for the Lord to do something in the person's interior life. For this reason I now feel uncomfortable in those meetings where people are falling over much like pins in a bowling alley, and then are

---

[30] *Interior Castle*, trans. by E. Allison Peers (Garden City, N.Y.; Image Books, 1961), p. 184.

quickly gotten to their feet, so the next person can come up and occupy their space. It's like the externals are magnified with no understanding of its real purpose.

In my experience it usually seems to happen after we have been praying for a while. If we are praying for people in a line, it may be the third or fourth person to whom it happens. Whatever this power is, it seems to increase after a period of prayer until it seems to fill the entire room, and occasionally people begin to be overcome by the Spirit, just as they stand there without anyone touching them. (I have seen this happen, upon occasion, to several priests gathered about the altar after a time of praise.) Moreover, a spirit of praise definitely increases the incidence of "resting in the Spirit."

When the people fall, they report it as being gentle and often experience a feeling of weightlessness. The following three excerpts from letters are typical accounts:

As you placed your hands very lightly on my forehead, then a feeling of weightlessness, as if I were on a cloud, came over me as I went down. There was this feeling of peace. Although I was semiconscious it was as if I were in another world which was very peaceful.

Then I got this feeling like I was falling and I could feel Father's hands grasping my head, as if to keep me from falling. Then I just went down like a feather, so softly. I felt weightless, but I was always conscious; I just had no control over my body. I wanted to get up, but I couldn't move, so I just stayed there, realizing for the first time in my life that Jesus loved me and forgave me my sins.

I was conscious and could vaguely hear when I chose to listen—but could not see or speak. When I heard the lady asking everybody to leave I tried to get up, but when I lifted up, my head was pulled back to the ground. There seemed to be a great weight on top of me which I was not conscious of until I tried to get up. When I tried to say, "I'm not able to leave," I discovered I could say no words except "Praise God," "Jesus" or pray in tongues. I was conscious of light shocks and twitches inside my head and body and a feeling of peace similar to an anaesthetic. I heard someone say "we are carrying you to another room"; I was conscious of being lifted but could do nothing to help. Eventually I sat up after being sort of "out of the body" for 45 minutes. I just had time to get to the terminal five minutes before the bus left for the plane I was to catch.

It is interesting to compare these descriptions with that of St. Teresa of Avila:

I can testify that after a rapture my body often seemed as light as if all weight had left it; sometimes this was so noticeable that I could hardly tell when my feet were touching the ground. For, while the rapture lasts, the body often remains dead and unable of itself to do anything; it continues all the time as it was when the rapture came upon it—in a sitting position, for example, or with the hands open or shut. The subject rarely loses consciousness; I have sometimes lost it altogether, but only seldom and for but a short time. As a rule the consciousness is disturbed; and though incapable of action with respect to outward things, the subject can still hear and understand, but only dimly, as though from a long way off....

There is very little, then, that a person in this condition can do, and this means that there will be little for him to do when the faculties come together again. Anyone, therefore, to whom the Lord grants this favour must not be discouraged at finding himself in this state, with the body unable to move for hours on end and the understanding and the memory sometimes wandering. True, they are generally absorbed in the praises of God or in an attempt to comprehend and realize what has happened to them....

The reason I am expounding this at such great length is that I know that there are persons now, in this very place, to whom the Lord is granting these favours; and if those who are directing such persons have not themselves experienced them—more especially if they have no learning—they may think that, when enraptured, they ought to be as if dead. It is a shame that such suffering should be caused by confessors who do not understand this. . . . The position, then, is that, however hard I try, my body, for considerable periods, has not the strength to make it capable of movement: all its strength has been taken away by the soul. Often a person who was previously quite ill and troubled with severe pain finds himself in good health again, and even stronger than before, for what the soul receives in rapture is a great gift, and sometimes, as I say, the Lord is pleased that the body should have a share in it because of its obedience to the will of the soul. After the recovery of consciousness, if the rapture has been deep, the faculties may remain absorbed for a day or two, or even for as long as three days. . . .[31]

In no way do I imply that the people to whom this happens are as holy as St. Teresa but, as she herself says, these are gifts that are often given to the weak by God to draw them to himself.

When people are resting in the Spirit, their situation varies widely: some are able to get up, but just feel like resting and praying; some are unable to get up and yet are fully aware of all that is going on; some are so caught up in an inward reality that they are unaware of what's going on around them.

The degree, too, of inward experience varies widely— all the way from persons simply having a kind of rest (without much of anything going on inwardly) to something like being caught up into the seventh heaven as Paul was, or having a vision of the Trinity.

I have found, too, that this power of the Spirit can increase in a person as you pray; it's almost as if a glass is being filled, and at a certain point it is filled to the brim, and the person falls. This filling usually takes a bit of time, sometimes up to three or four minutes. So it seems to help if the person does not fall right away but waits until he has received as much of this power as possible—and then stays resting as long as it feels right.[32]

---

[31] *Life, op. cit.*, pp. 196-198.

[32] It's not the falling, after all, that's important: it's the filling with the power of the Spirit. Sometimes the person doesn't fall at all, but the effect is the same, as in this letter:

I really never thought I would have the "hysterical reaction"

I have found that this being overcome by the Spirit, in our meetings anyway, is always peaceful, always decorous. (I have seen documentary movies of various Pentecostal churches where people fall to the ground and roll or twitch. I don't understand what goes on in those meetings, and I don't feel at all comfortable with seeing it.) Maybe one out of 10 persons we pray with starts crying, or there is some kind of emotional eruption. All the instances of this that I know lead me to believe that the power of the Spirit has touched upon a need for inner healing or deliverance. The need for inner healing usually comes forth in tears that have often been left uncried for many years. If we minister with that person for a time, the inner healing takes place, usually in an easier way than when the power of the Spirit is not as manifestly present. Occasionally, if evil spirits are present, the power of the Spirit stirs them up; they can't stand that degree of the power of the Spirit, so they surface. Again, when this happens, we can take the person to a place where we have the privacy to minister and finish the deliverance. In short, anything which is not simple and peaceful is not the direct action of the Spirit, but is the *reaction* of wounded human nature or the forces of evil.

In London, for instance, in the summer of 1975, as I was walking into Westminster Hall where Fountain Trust was holding a large conference, a young woman stopped me and, after introducing herself as a fellow American, asked if I could pray for inner healing. I

---

some before me in the chapel line had had   the falling back and the tears   because I am a non-hysterical type. However, when I asked you to pray I experienced a deep sense as of fire burning through me, tingling throughout my veins, trembling as from too much pressure, and very weak knees. Actually, if left a bit longer, I would also have fallen. I left you, dazed, staggering, tearful, and went to sit quietly, thankfully in the middle of the chapel. I stayed there until 11:45 p.m. and finally had to leave. I was praying throughout, mostly in wonder and thanks of God's great, immense gifts to me—especially himself.

It continued all night; I found myself in the same state three times, for long periods.... Today it is still with me, a sense of his being with me and utter surrender to him. (It is now 4 p.m.)

explained to her that there really wasn't time to pray adequately before going in to hear the talk. But as we got into the hall, I noticed a large side room, and I asked if she and the woman who accompanied her would just like to pray briefly in the little time we had. Although there wasn't enough time to pray for inner healing, still I thought the Lord might work in an exceptional way if we prayed briefly in tongues. After all, God knew our limitations. She was eager to pray, so we ducked into the room and I prayed briefly. She was overcome in the Spirit—much to her own and her friend's surprise—but then she began to tremble and moan. In her case, a deliverance had begun; the prayer took two hours, and we came out at the same time the crowd was letting out of the hall. We missed the talk, but she was freed of anxieties and problems that had plagued her for years. Her father, a minister, wrote me three months later to say that an extraordinary transformation had come over his daughter.

Because of these helpful experiences, I have come to see that this "overcoming in the Spirit" can be a real help in ministry in a way that I have never seen it used by evangelists, except in the descriptions I have read in the Hunters' book, *Since Jesus Passed By*. If I feel it is appropriate (usually because I don't have the time to go through a full prayer for inner healing or deliverance), I just explain "resting in the Spirit" briefly to the person, so he or she won't be surprised if it should happen, and then inwardly ask for Jesus to fill the person with his life and power. Then if it does happen, the people can rest for as long as they wish, from a few seconds to several hours; and when they get up, I can talk to them and find out what happened inwardly and see if any further prayer is needed.

DANGERS

Clearly, in all this, there can be problems, principally because it appears so sensational and people understand it so little.[33] It's something like the gift of tongues when it was quite new; people are impressed because it is so different, so sensation-seeking can easily take over. Hopefully, when resting in the Spirit is better known, its spiritual purpose will become central, and it will no longer cause astonishment. But the answer to most of these problems is not *suppression*—in which case its value and purpose are lost to the community—but its wise use until it becomes so well understood that its sensational aspects are minimized, in much the same way as praying in tongues is accepted as a matter of course in charismatic prayer meetings. Nevertheless, until that time (and even after) there are some real problems:

1) *Sensationalism.*

People being what they are, they tend to look for the novel and spectacular. Instead of looking for Jesus, they look for observable results. Often, when people are falling over right and left, a circus atmosphere results that will bother any reflective Christian. Last year, after one meeting where a woman evangelist seemed to take delight

---

[33] Father George Maloney (*op. cit.*) warns about the dangers of people seeking the experience rather than seeking God. I don't see these two as divided; what I find is that people are mostly seeking an experience of God, and that they are helped to love God by this experience. The following letter is typical of those I receive:

... I experienced a deep peace and it seemed as if I were floating. I was totally overcome by the Spirit, I have never in my life experienced Jesus so beautifully. Ever since, my relationship with Jesus really has grown and I have a new awareness of him, whether at school, home, or wherever. And I know this isn't meant to be an experience and then it's over. I know it is meant that I grow constantly more aware of his presence in my life.

Father Maloney also warns against hysteria and a mingling of natural suggestibility, confusing it with the action of the Holy Spirit. This is a real danger; all I can say is that, at our meetings there is always great peace; and when I talk to people afterwards, I find that the sense of the presence of God has been heightened. In short, the fruits are good. The times when there is agitation and disturbance usually seem to result from individuals who are emotionally or spiritually disturbed; they can be counseled or prayed with privately.

in seeing people fall, a Jewish observer told me that it seemed like witchcraft to her. Newspapers don't help either; reporters naturally tend to pick out noteworthy externals and describe them at great length, and pass over any more ordinary happenings there may be in the meeting. I don't blame the reporters, because they are looking for what is newsworthy, for what is different and for what can be described in visual terms. It's just that balance can disappear—both at the meeting and in any description of the meeting given to those who were not there.

2) *Not always a sign of the Spirit.*

There are psychic and natural counterparts of this phenomenon, and it is a mistake to make the easy judgment (which I'm afraid some people make) that

- a) a *meeting* is more "Spirit-filled" where this takes place,
- b) a *minister* is more spiritual through whose hands people are "slain in the Spirit." Some of the people I have met in whose ministry this takes place have not particularly impressed me as persons.

Similarly, I have heard of a pastor, some of whose teaching I would regard as false (he asks Catholics who come to his church to smash their statues and rip up their rosaries), who has a real healing ministry where people are often overcome by the Spirit. Catholics are confused, because they figure "God must be with him to do these works of power; so what he teaches must be true."

All I can say is that similar things happen when I pray for people, but I don't expect that everything I preach is *necessarily* true; the truth of anything I preach is a separate issue and subject to the judgment of the Church and the community.

- c) "A person who is overcome in the Spirit is more spiritual than someone who does not yield."

Some people I know who have not been overcome when they were prayed for seem to me to be very close to the Lord. Perhaps the reason it did not happen was that they were already so accustomed to the power of the Spirit that there was very little differential in power, as it were. St. Teresa of Avila says that as she grew accustomed to the power of God, the bodily manifestations *became less* as her prayer life became stronger.

Of interest here, Blessed Henry Suso, a 14th-century Dominican mystic, writes (presumably about a vision he himself experienced):

> A certain devout man asked God to favor him with a spiritual festival. In a subsequent vision the thirty-year-old Christ entered the man's room, asked him for a glass of wine, and offered a drink to three persons who had come with him. The first took a drink and sank to the floor in a swoon; the second became slightly dizzy; the third was not at all affected by the draught. Then Christ explained that this occurrence signified the different effects produced by divine consolation on beginning, progressing, and perfect men.[34]

It seems then that people who are accustomed to spiritual experiences are less likely to be overcome by the Spirit. Moreover, some critics of the phenomenon claim that the people most likely to fall are suggestible kinds of people teenagers, for instance. Now, that's true, I think. A teenager is far more likely to fall than a 70-year-old nun in full habit.

But it is not all that simple. My experience leads me to believe that, generally, a person who is open to the Spirit whether mature or immature is more likely than not to rest in the Spirit. The sign of maturity or

---

[34] *The Exemplar: Life and Writings of Blessed Henry Suso, O.P.* (trans. by Sister M. Ann Edward, O.P.), Vol. I (Dubuque, Iowa; Priory Press, 1962), pp. 108-109.

immaturity is not whether they fall or not, but *how* they respond: The mature rest in a great peace and tranquillity; the immature with a certain amount of manifest emotion, such as laughter or joy. In my mind it is a plus to be the kind of person who might rest in the Spirit; it isn't just a question of suggestibility—although for some people that factor does enter in. Many people actually fight not to be overcome and yet when the power (whatever it is) is very strong, they still fall.

There are certain types of people who seem to block this experience—notably those who lead lives where they have overcontrolled their emotions. Some people are really afraid to let go. It isn't so much a spiritual problem as an emotional one; they are afraid of anything they can't control through their reason. Some people seem to be mature, but they are really overcontrolled and have lost their ability to respond to life with spontaneity.

In short, it is foolhardy to make any kind of general judgment about the people who are overcome in the Spirit as distinct from those who are not. Some fall because they are immature and are just looking for some kind of experience; others refuse to fall, because they are emotionally restricted (and immature in a different way). Some people are overcome by the Spirit because they are open and yield to the Spirit; others don't fall because they are already so close to God that there is no differential that would cause them to fall. On the other hand, some who I believe are very close to the Lord and sensitive to the inspirations of the Spirit often rest in the Spirit at our meetings. So "judge not that you be not judged."[35]

---

[35] "In regard to the inebriation of love, one should take great care not to confuse this effect of the prayer of quiet with a purely natural effervescence and sentimentality, which are often found in enthusiastic and impressionable individuals. And even if it is a question of a true phenomenon, the soul should not willingly let itself be carried away by this experience, but should strive to control and moderate it. Above all, one should not take this phenomenon as a sign that it is far advanced in the spiritual life, but should humble itself before God and never seek to practice prayer in order to obtain consolations from God." (Antonio Royo, *The Theology of Christian Perfection*, trans. by Jordan Aumann, O.P. (Dubuque, IA; Priory Press, 1964), p. 545.)

3) *Pride.*

At some meetings where I've seen much "slaying in the Spirit," it seems to me that some people have been pushed who were not on the point of falling on their own. And I have to admit that when I have been praying and several people, one after the other, have fallen, and then one doesn't go down, I begin to wonder to myself, "Why doesn't this person go down?" It is so easy to judge, to strive for effect!

I also confess that when there are several lines, I begin to look over at the other lines and, almost instinctively, I compare. If more externally is happening in another line, I may experience an inner envy, even though on the conscious level, I believe everything I have written earlier about these phenomena not being a sign of holiness either in myself or in the persons I am praying for. I don't like to admit these things, but, as St. Francis de Sales said, pride will only disappear 15 minutes after we die. Because of this temptation to vanity, the minister of healing may be inwardly using a kind of *psychic* force, desiring the person to go down, which may have its effect, but it will not be of God. Always when I am ministering, I need to pray to free myself (and everyone else) from any kind of spiritual striving, so I will not be relying on any effort or upon mere psychological energy. I think it quite possible that some ministers of healing are dealing more in human psychological powers than in the power of the Spirit.

4) *Not everyone is healed.*

At times, when I have prayed for people to be healed and they have been overcome in the Spirit, they have not been healed. They may have had an experience of peace, or they may have even had some kind of deep spiritual union with God, but that still doesn't necessarily mean they have been physically or emotionally healed. It probably shouldn't be necessary to say this after everything else I have written about people not being healed, but so many people are disappointed when their expectations don't immediately come true, that it's important to help them to accept the inward blessing of peace that they have received through resting in the Spirit and not lose this blessing through anxiety or false guilt about not receiving something else.

Nevertheless, resting in the Spirit seems to be a state in which it is more likely than usual that a person will receive an inner healing or physical healing. At times it almost seems as if it is like an operation where the person is put to rest for God's surgery—at times, the surgery is brief; at other times it is a six-hour operation.

WHY SAY ANYTHING ABOUT IT?

When this first began to happen in my ministry, I was concerned about saying anything because of all the problems of a circus-type atmosphere that I foresaw. When I would notice that this phenomenon was beginning, I would stop praying with the person, or I would only pray with people who were sitting down.

After a number of people, though, shared with me their interior experience while they were resting in the Spirit, I came to the conclusion that I might be inhibiting what God wanted to do to help people, because of my own timidity and desire for respectability. I also saw that people who had never seen this before might be afraid and disturbed if no explanation were given. Consequently, when I think some in a group will be overcome, I explain the phenomenon before we pray, but I try to do this briefly, so as not to center their attention upon externals. Furthermore, I am conscious that the power of suggestion could be at work in all this, and I don't want to induce any of these phenomena in a purely psychological way.[36] At other times, I say nothing to a group beforehand. If it starts, then I explain it.

Even knowing that some critics may say that, by mentioning it beforehand, I am using suggestion and setting the stage for people to be overcome by the Spirit, I

---

[36] I think it is noteworthy that the authors of several of the letters quoted in this chapter had never heard of being overcome in the Spirit until it happened to them.

have come to the conclusion that it is still better to speak about it than not.

For one thing, if it does happen without preparation, then I will have to say something about it eventually, so why not now? If people don't understand it, they may resist it out of fear when it begins to happen to them. It is possible to resist and prevent its taking place most of the time. If this should happen, the person will lose whatever benefit he or she might have received.

Also, the bystanders may not understand and will become concerned. It is important to let people resting in the Spirit remain as long as they wish without interruption. Unless bystanders are acquainted with the phenomenon, they are likely to think that those overcome have fainted and may try to revive them and get them to sit up. Recently I was present when concerned relatives were trying to get a woman to sit up while she was asking them to just leave her alone.

Furthermore, you need to ask one or two people to stand behind the people you pray for, to ease them to the floor should they fall.[37]

Another thing to keep in mind—if this happens when people are sitting down, their heads tend to go back (sometimes forward), and it hurts the neck. This will wake them again, as it were. Or they may feel that they have to hold themselves on the chair. Again, this need to exert themselves and turn their attention to the outward order will inhibit any interior experience from taking place. If I feel that this "resting in the Spirit" may take place as we minister to people, I pray for people standing, rather than sitting. If I think that a sufficient reason exists for not wanting people to be overcome (e.g., too many observers who wouldn't understand), I pray for people in a sitting position, and I desist as soon as I see the person start to slump.

I have to admit that in writing this chapter I feel somewhat ridiculous. Some readers who have not seen

---

[37] If I decide not to say anything about it, I stand to the side of the persons when I pray so that my right hand can pillow their heads in case they fall back.

people overcome in the Spirit may think I have spent too much time on such an unusual subject—a side issue. But like so many things which up to now have been unusual and restricted to certain unique individual ministries, I now see it spreading in the Catholic charismatic renewal. It's as if gifts are given community-wide now instead of being limited to individuals. And since so little has been written about the meaning of resting in the Spirit, it seemed important to share some reflections to help all those who have experienced it in their own ministry.

As with most phenomena, it would be a great mistake to do anything to induce it. On the other hand, when it is genuine and the Spirit seems to be guiding it, it would be a mistake to prevent its taking place, unless there is a serious reason for doing so.

The basic reason for the body's falling is, as the Dominican theologian Antonio Royo wrote, because "the human organism can react in only a certain number of ways, and when the spirit is absorbed in an intense activity, the body necessarily participates in this activity."[38] But he also cautions, following St. John of the Cross, that these startling reactions in the body usually occur only in beginners.[39]

I have seen such powerful healings take place when a person is overcome in the Spirit, that I see it as a wonderful aid to the healing ministry if and when God should choose to give it as his free gift. It's as if the Lord himself moves in and works far more than we can ever hope or imagine. As I have said, it is always peaceful, except in those cases where the power of God meets deep hurts in the person (or, occasionally, evil spirits) and opens them out where they can be healed more quickly than ordinarily.

I have seen every kind of healing take place while people were resting in the Spirit—all the way from physical healing to the deepest spiritual transformation. Let me conclude with two such testimonies, one of a

---

[38] *Op. cit.*, p. 536.
[39] *Loc. cit.*

physical healing, the other of a spiritual transformation that included inner healing, deliverance and physical healing:

1.

After the experience, all pain, muscle spasms, tensions and pressures in my head, neck, arm, shoulder, upper and lower back and right leg were completely gone. The following five days, totally free of any kind of discomfort, was the longest period of such freedom from pain, etc., since the car accident 11 years ago. Since the end of those five days, varying degrees of muscle spasms, tension and pressures that result in the buildup of pain have returned, but the pain is greatly lessened as are all the other symptoms. My husband and I pray for the continued fullness of his healing power every day. Sometimes, after praying, the pain will again go completely. My doctor, an orthopedic surgeon, who has been treating me every other week for a year and a half, confirmed last week a "100 percent improvement" in the condition of all areas. For the first time since coming to him when I was in acute chronic muscle spasm with three vertebrae, seven discs, both left and right sacroiliac pulled out, causing leg and arm nerve damage, this last visit—everything was in place! The first and second layers of muscle were relaxed to the point that for the first time he could reach and work with the most severely injured third layer of muscles in my neck and shoulder! And a blocked nerve damage that had resisted any treatment was healed, freeing the use of my right thumb.

The doctor spoke about my experience as having in some way been the source of accelerated healing, and that the days that followed free from all pain, was a time of the body being taught how to be free of spasm, etc. He believes now the healing will progress more rapidly to a completion than it probably ever could have before.

2.

When I came to you asking for healing, I knew that I needed inner healing. In fact, all the four types you mention in your book. I was most concerned with inner healing and deliverance. I was so heavily burdened and weighed down with so much pain that I couldn't see straight or think clearly. All I knew was that I was hurting and bleeding inside.

When I think of how much junk and chaos was inside me; I was weighed down by my sins and ready to blow my mind away, even questioning my own sanity. The hypocrisy of my life was getting to me smiling on the outside, pretending that everything was O.K., while deep inside I was hurting.

And now to feel so light and free freer than the birds singing with crazy versatility just outside my window, more joyful than the song they are singing, happy to be alive, soooo happy, no longer having to pretend, just free to be me, free to move around, and most of all, free to love everyone, especially those I live with. What an exhilarating experience of being once more with Jesus. And now I know why and what it means to be a Sister, to be singled out just for Jesus. What a joy to be *all* his!

Appendix I
When and
When Not to Pray

One of the most difficult things for people to believe is that they should expect great things to happen when they pray for healing. The next most difficult thing— once they have belief—seems to be that there are times when they should not pray for healing of sick friends or relatives. Two perceptive essays have been written on this subject; I was so impressed in reading them that I wanted to include them in this book so that more people might share their wisdom.

The first essay is by Dr. Charles Farah, Jr., Professor of Theological and Historical Studies at Oral Roberts University (Tulsa, Oklahoma), and is a straightforward presentation of the vitally important difference between *logos*, the word of God as an objective, general principle, and *rayma*, the word of God addressed to us to act upon. The confusion of these two understandings of "word of God" is what leads to many of the pastoral problems people experience in trying to "claim their healings" when God has not spoken to them.

The second selection is taken from Graham Pulkingham's book, *They Left Their Nets* (New York: Morehouse-Barlow, 1973), and is a moving example of the anguish caused when people attempt to proclaim God's will in regard to healing when they don't really have God's guidance. It is a perfect example of the devastation caused in human lives when they fail to understand the distinction Dr. Farah makes in his essay. This personal account of the anguish suffered by a young man when his wife dies of cancer is so poignant that I have never managed to read it in public without being moved to tears.

A. Faith or Presumption
by Dr. Charles Farah, Jr.[1]

Lives all over the Christian community have been wrecked by a bad theology. It says, among other things: Miracles are not for today; the enemy cannot bother a Christian, he is off limits; everyone who is prayed for must be healed since the only condition for healing is faith. And on it goes.

Listen to some classic words of bad theology:

> Then the devil took Him into the holy city; and he stood Him on the pinnacle of the temple, and said to Him, "If You are the Son of God, throw Yourself down; for it is written, *'He will give His angels charge concerning you; and on their hands they will bear you up, lest you strike your foot against a stone'*" (Mt 4:5-6 NAS).

In this passage of scripture we see the enemy tempting Jesus. Satan, the master of temptation, had recourse to any temptation he wanted to use—the sins of the sense or spiritual pride   but he chose the sin of presumption. It is strange we do not hear more about the sin of presumption, because it is one of the most prevalent problems in the body of Christ.

The devil said, "If you are the Son of God, then prove it, jump off the temple." This was a short cut! A way to win the instant allegiance of the people. Jesus was on the defensive. Satan knew Jesus' strong point was the word of God, so he quoted a proof text to back up his statement,

---

[1] Dr. Charles Farah, Jr., Professor of Theological and Historical Studies at Oral Roberts University, is a leader in the charismatic renewal. He holds degrees from Wheaton College, Fuller Theological Seminary and a Ph.D. from the University of Edinburgh in Scotland, and has served on the Board of Directors for the Christian Renewal Ministry since its inception.

". . . He will give His angels charge over you. . . ." Here is the sin of presumption.

I thank God for a sound tradition which says you need more than one text of scripture, you need the *whole* counsel of God. For proper guidance we need to know and understand all that God has to say on a subject. The devil knows the bible backwards and forwards and he knows hows how to get us in trouble with it.

Notice how carefully the devil quoted Psalm 91:11-12. He says, "He shall give His angels charge concerning you," but he carefully omits the phrase which follows, ". . . to guard you in all your ways." This phrase qualifies the verse by saying that God will guard you in all your *ordinary* ways of life. But without this phrase Satan can turn it into a universal and say, "You can climb up on the temple and jump down and expect God to take care of you."

Satan wanted Jesus to believe, as he would us, that he could do anything he wished and God would have to take care of him. The Lord has allowed many of us to live with the tragedy of our mistakes. We find out that God's protection does not necessarily apply in *all* situations.

On the other side of the sin of presumption is the sin of unbelief. In between is the golden mean of faith. Jesus lived in the realm of faith. So when the devil tempted him, Jesus, knowing the whole counsel of God, answered, "On the other hand, it is written, 'You shall not tempt the Lord your God'" (Mt 4:7 NAS). He was saying that by casting himself off the temple he would be committing the sin of presumption in tempting the Lord God. Not even he, the Son of God, had that right.

Many times we have been guilty of playing the devil's advocate by telling people to jump off the temple. "I've prayed for you, now take off your glasses, you're healed. It doesn't make any difference if your driver's license says you must wear them and you still can't see." Or, "Since you have been prayed for, you are healed of diabetes. Don't take your insulin even though the symptoms are still there. The symptoms are lies." I have seen lying symptoms turned into harsh reality, doing great damage to the cause of Christ. This is why we must come to understand the whole counsel of God.

RAYMA AND LOGOS

There are two Greek words which should throw a little light on the difference between "faith" and "presumption." One is the word *rayma;* the other is the word *logos.* Both of these words are translated in the New Testament as "word." Karl Barth speaks of this difference as "the word of God *to you,* which is *rayma,* and the word of God, *logos,* which is *universal.*"

Romans 10:17, which is so freely quoted, says, "So faith comes by hearing, and hearing by the word of Christ." In Greek it is "the *rayma* of Christ," which is the word of God *to you.* Let me illustrate what this means. How many of you became Christians the very first time that you heard the gospel? I dare say you heard it many times before you repented and believed. There was one moment in your life when God spoke a word to you and it sank into your spirit. The *logos* became a *rayma.*

The bible, the Ten Commandments, the gospels are all *logos*—the universal word of God to all men. Jesus Christ is the final *logos* to all men everywhere. He never changes, he is the same. But before the *logos* can do us any good, it must become *rayma.* Some of you may have read the bible yet it never meant a thing to you. It was *logos.* Then one day it came alive—it was *to you, rayma.*

We can apply this to three areas which are often troublesome in finding balance in the life of the believer: Guidance, Healing and Prophecy.

GUIDANCE

We are usually not very advanced in the Christian life until we realize that the word of the Lord which is spoken *to us* may not be the word of the Lord which is given to another person. God's guidance for me is not the same as it is for my friends.

There are two wonderful examples of this in the New

Testament. The first is in Matthew 14:22-33, where we find the story of Peter walking on the water. The disciples had been through a rough day ministering to the multitudes. Toward evening Jesus made them take their boat and start home across the Sea of Galilee while he went off to pray. The boat had not gotten far out when it was hit by a storm. The disciples rowed for all they were worth, but they did not seem to have much success against the wind and the waves.

To make things even worse, a ghost showed up about three o'clock in the morning. Frightened, they began to panic and yell with fear, but Jesus said, "Don't be afraid, it's me!"

Peter became a little bolder at this point and challenged, "Lord, if it is really you, tell me to come to you." (I don't really think Peter had any idea of walking on the water, but he asked anyway.) Jesus answered him, "Come." Now here is the point of the whole story. Who came to Jesus on the water? *Peter*. None of the other disciples jumped overboard to join in the fun only Peter. They were quite happy to let him go it alone. When Christ said, "Come," it was clearly a *rayma* for Peter and no one else.

Christians have never taken this verse and said, "The scripture clearly teaches from this that we don't need boats, we can all walk on the water." That would be absurd because it was a *rayma* for Peter and no one else.

The second such incident again involves Peter and is found in John 21:18-22. Looking very briefly at this passage we find that Jesus is with his disciples by the Sea of Galilee one morning after his resurrection. Sitting at breakfast, Jesus turned to Peter and said, "I have a word for you. The day is going to come when you are going to be crucified and you are not going to want to be. Now, follow me."

Peter asked Jesus, "What about my friend, John?"

Jesus told him, "John is none of your business, follow me."

Jesus' *rayma* to Peter was not intended to be his *rayma* to John. He had a word for each of them and all they had to worry about was following their shepherd. Your guidance and my guidance may not be the same, but the thing which we have in common is hearing the voice of the shepherd.

I learned while visiting Scotland how really dumb sheep are. Believe me, it is no compliment to be called a sheep. They get themselves caught in fences; if one jumps off a cliff, the rest will follow. But in spite of their stupidity, the sheep do know how to follow their master's voice. It is the voice of the master that we must learn to hear in this matter of guidance.

It may be God's word (*logos*), but is it God's word word (*rayma*) to me? We can begin to harangue the Lord, "Lord, it's in your word, you've got to do it, it's in the book!" That is what the devil did, "It's in the book, Jesus. If you believe the book, you'll jump off the temple." It is possible for us to set our beliefs above God himself. We say, "God, it's there in the book, it's got to happen." You may discover, as I did, that it does not always happen. I have argued with God when things did not go according to the rules. "God, if I had a son who was doing all he could to serve you, I wouldn't have treated him like you've treated me!" I forgot how God treated his Son. What God does to us may not always be "fair."

Man's glory is to walk upright and gaze into heaven and argue his case with his Creator. But his glory can also be his mistake as it was with Job's theologians. They had God boxed in with their little syllogisms. They said: A godly man does not suffer. Job, you are suffering. Therefore, you are not godly. Bad theology! Formulas scare me to death. Do you remember how Job and his friends ended up? When Job saw God he said, ". . . Now my eye sees you. Wherefore I abhor myself and repent in dust and ashes."

Then God told Job, "Make an offering for your friends, they have sinned *presumptuously* against me." The sin of presumption—putting God in your little box.

I lived for a time in the book of Job and the message God gave me through that time was his sovereignty. The secret of Job is in Job 33:12. It says simply, "God is greater than man." God does as he wills and no one can stay his hand.

We need to understand our place under the sovereignty of God. When Jesus came to the end of the road at Gethsemane, he knelt and prayed. When we as Christians kneel in prayer for guidance, there must come a higher prayer than, "What is fair?" or "Why is this happening to me?" We need to ask, "What is your will, Lord?" And when we come to the place where Jesus came in Gethsemane, we need to bow our heads and say, "Not my will, but thine be done."

HEALING

Healing has caused severe problems because many of the things which are supposed to work do not bring the desired results. Sometimes people are healed, sometimes they are not.

The arguments run like this: Is healing in the atonement? Isaiah 53:4, "Surely our sicknesses he himself bore and our pains he carried ... by his scourging we are healed." No question—healing is in the atonement. With this in mind we box God into our little syllogism that goes like this: Healing is in the atonement. Faith is the key that unlocks the healing of Jesus. Since I have prayed for you in faith, you are healed, right? Not necessarily so. There are other factors that enter into the picture.

It is a great tragedy that we have placed so many of God's children under condemnation because we have told them, "You were not healed because you did not have the faith."

A friend of mine went into the home where a little girl was dying of leukemia—he had the *logos*. It was in the book, she would be healed. He told the parents not to worry about a thing, prayed for the little girl and went out praising God. Three weeks later the little girl was dead. My friend went into a spiritual tailspin for six months.

I recently returned from a city where one of our young graduates from Oral Roberts University was emerging from a shattering spiritual experience.

A man had joined his church who practiced a brand of theology which says: Faith, if exercised, would always save the sick. This man prayed for a fine Spirit-filled, Christian professor who was a diabetic and told him, "You are healed, get off your insulin." This was on a Thursday and by Sunday the man was almost dead. The wife was frantic with fear. When the man who practiced this type of "faith" returned to the home, he found the wife on the floor and began casting demons out of her. He said to the professor, who was approaching death, "You are going to be all right." My friend finally took over and got the professor to a hospital an hour away from death. He was convinced that this man would have let him die.

Bad theology is a cruel taskmaster. If, however, God speaks a *rayma* to you, you can be sure it will come to pass.

Some time back a young wife of a professor at Oral Roberts University called my wife. She had just returned from a visit to her doctor and was quite shaken. After the doctor had finished all his tests he told her, "You have an obstruction in your heart. We don't know how great it is, but this obstruction has to be viewed and we are going to give you an angiogram. This procedure itself can induce a heart attack. You must understand the dangers that are involved."

When she called my wife immediately there was a word, a *rayma*, spoken to my heart. "Honey, she is going to be all right," I said. We went over and spent an evening with her and her husband and together we were refreshed in the spirit. After we had prayed, she asked, "Do you still believe I am going to be all right?"

"You are going to be all right," I answered.

During the night my wife and I were awakened individually to intercede and pray for her. The next day president Roberts came over to see her. He told her, "I didn't need to come, you are going to be all right." The word had been confirmed by the witness of two.

That night in the hospital she faced the terror of a serious operation the following morning. I cannot explain it, I only know God let me feel that terror, and I prayed specifically that when they did the angiogram there would be no terror for her. God answered and she had perfect rest.

When the doctor came in after the operation he said that it looked very encouraging. They had found nothing. Confirming it with X-rays, he reported there was absolutely no obstruction. There was no explanation. Her heart was perfect, and he sent her home.

Now that was a *rayma*. We did not need 29 verses of "Only Believe" to work up faith. It was a gift from God. I had nothing to do with it. How do we know this was a *rayma*? Because the facts proved it. God was at work. He spoke and he healed.

When we tell people, "You are healed," we had better be sure that we have a word from God. Many times people are healed because they exercise faith in God, but Mark 11:22 tells us that there is the faith *of* God. When God speaks a *rayma* it is from his own mountain-moving faith and it is unshakable, no matter what the circumstances are. This kind of faith is from a sovereign almighty God.

PROPHECY

Prophecy normally falls into the category of *rayma* since it is a word for a particular time and situation. This is why we must be most careful about publishing magazines full of prophecies. These prophecies, however valid, were given by God to a particular assembly for a particular time and situation, and are not necessarily meant to be universal prophecies.

Prophecies circulated around from group to group may be listened to, if they witness to your spirit, but the normal means of receiving a prophetic word is found in 1 Corinthians 14. It is to be given to a specific congregation and judged by others. Such words given to other groups may not fit what is happening in your own congregation.

Often we do not know it, but we are speaking a word of prophecy. I was in Jacksonville, Florida, staying in the home of a Presbyterian minister and his wife. In the course of a conversation one evening on healing, I told them, "Sir, you may have a backache and your wife may have arthritis, but when the Lord heals, it will be a gift of healing to each of you."

Later when they had both beautifully received the baptism in the Holy Spirit, the wife told me, "One of the factors in our receiving the baptism was what you said about my arthritis and my husband's backaches. There was no way you could have known except from God." It was a word of knowledge, even though I did not know it at the time. This is what I Corinthians 14:25 means when it says, "The secrets of a man's heart will be revealed."

Personal prophecy is the area in which we most generally find difficulty. I would venture to say that 60 percent to 70 percent of the personal prophecies which have come to me in my life have not proved true. Many of them had to do with specific times and details. We often hear people say, "I want a word of prophecy from this person or that person." Often the word of the Lord is "Wait on me," and we never hear it because we are so busy running around.

Do not take this wrongly. I have received and believe in personal prophecy. The other day one of the elders in our group brought a prophecy which said to beware of Elymas the Sorcerer when I went to a certain place. I arrived at that place and sure enough there was Elymas the Sorcerer—only it was a woman. That word of prophecy was an aid to help me receive understanding in a given situation. Prophecy is meant to be *confirmatory* rather than directive.

In the Church the Spirit is in the *community* of believers and the community of believers has the right to judge prophecy. It will be necessary occasinally to judge the prophecies that come and reject those that are not of the spirit of the meeting.

One time during a beautiful spirit of praise a young lady brought a prophecy that was terribly condemnatory. She said, "You must likewise repent or go to hell."

I had to say, "I'm sorry but we do not accept that prophecy as coming from the Lord." The lady and her bevy of followers got up and left. That proved that it was not from the Lord, because the body is given the right to judge.

If someone has a word for you, ask if they mind if you put it before the body to be judged. If he refuses, he is not a true prophet. A true prophet will say, "Of course, let's judge it." If it is received, then it is true prophecy.

The Lord is calling us to live lives of sober integrity, to begin to hear his voice in these three areas. Jesus was tempted, as are we, by the sin of presumption, but he did not succumb. We must learn to distinguish between the *logos* which is universal, eternal and objective; and the *rayma* which is particular, temporal and subjective.

B. A Husband's Perplexity
by William Farra[1]

For about six months she had been confused. On the advice of those who believed she was physically healed, she had begun to anticipate that the eventual accomplishment of the miracle would be a testimony to Houston churches, many of which rejected spiritual healing. She had been exhorted not to look at the empirical evidence of her disease but to the promises of God. If Shirley could state with her lips that she had been healed when there were still obvious symptoms, she would be showing a strong faith. God would vindicate that by the eventual fact of her healing.

Of course Shirley wanted to be healed, and she had asked God to do so. But the promise he had quickened to her mind at the moment of the leukemia diagnosis was a word of simple assurance in His power to draw her to Himself. On others' advice she had tried to claim a healing, but the attempt felt less than honest. She was

---

[1] This account of the conflicting advice given to William Farra when it was discovered that his wife, Shirley, had leukemia, is taken from W. Graham Pulkingham's book, *They Left Their Nets* (New York; Morehouse-Barlow, 1973), pp. 77-85 passim. Used by permission of publisher.

caught between dishonesty and faithlessness when she wanted neither; hence the confusion. . . .

Three weeks after my baptism in the Spirit, Shirley was again hospitalized with a high fever. It was Friday and I went to the prayer meeting at Church of the Redeemer to solicit their prayers. Her fever vanished in the night. But while we rejoiced some disappointing news came: the doctors were keeping her there for observation. The cancerous white cells, once again developing immunity to current medications, had multiplied rapidly and the research staff must find a new drug. One experiment after another failed and Shirley's body was at the mercy of its destructive foe.

The days of that period of hospitalization were for me a physical and emotional marathon. I managed to bear up under the weight of my other commitments, but the only thing that really mattered was Shirley. A losing battle with leukemia became the preoccupation of our lives as we whirled together in a kaleidoscope of thoughts and feelings that were usually intense and often perplexing.

Shirley had been in the hospital for about a month when Graham Pulkingham phoned saying he wanted to talk with me as soon as possible. . . .

When I reached the church he was waiting in his office and we greeted each other in an exchange of pleasantries. Offering me a chair he arranged one for himself facing me. Plainly there was something serious to be said.

"Bill," he began, "there are people in the parish who keep up with Shirley's condition, you know, and last Friday at the chapel service a woman told us how bleak things are right now. She asked us to take a stand of faith with Shirley's friends who believe God will raise her up and restore her to health. That caused a little confusion in me, Bill, because I wasn't sure what the Lord wanted. It's God's mercy that I trust. If He gives me a special nudge about Shirley's healing I'll gladly speak about that. But in the absence of a special word I can only trust His mercy."

I assured him I knew the confusion because I'd been in the middle of it for a month.

"I thought it was time to face the confusion head on, Bill, so I suggested that everyone who could, begin fasting and ask the Lord to clear the air a bit. I wanted to know how to pray for Shirley. About forty of us started fasting last Saturday morning and we kept it up till Monday."

Graham's voice was soft and he spoke slowly, picking his words. He was looking me full in the face.

"There's a woman in St. Louis named Kathleen Thomerson," he continued. "She played the organ here for a while last summer and got baptized with the Spirit at the same time.

"Last Monday she called me and her first words were, 'Graham are you fasting?' You can imagine my surprise. For a couple of days she'd been having strange thoughts and turning up unusual scriptures, but she didn't want to be misled so she asked the Lord somehow to show her if they weren't reliable. When she asked for a sign He indicated we were fasting, so she decided to call me and find out."

I began sensing the gravity of Graham's words.

"When I told her to go ahead, she said she'd been praying last Friday and Saturday and kept remembering scriptures about the way God is glorified by death. She mentioned several places in the Bible, like the death of Lazarus and Stephen's stoning—other places, too. When she felt an urge to share these scriptures with me she couldn't understand why, so she prayed some more, and on Sunday something pretty positive happened. Mind you, she doesn't know you or Shirley, Bill, but the Lord gave her the name Shirley—sort of out of the blue."

Graham leaned forward and put his hand on my knee. The tone of his voice was earnest but gentle. "Bill, I don't know how to say this except straight out. The Lord told Kathleen we were praying for Shirley's healing, but He wants us to release her to Him so He can take her home."

The words my heart feared had been spoken.

For a few breathless seconds my eyes were fixed on Graham's face. Then suddenly I felt the emotional impact of what he had been saying and it was as if Shirley were already gone. Tears of grief poured down my face.

Graham moved close and I clung to him for a very long time, heaving and sobbing.

Outside the church I wept again. Going quickly to the privacy of my car I wept with a lonely mourning and agonized before God. Why, Lord, why?

"He wants us to release her . . . take her home." Words that rang true—but impossible to contemplate!

When the first shock of Graham's words passed, confusion was gone too; for the first time in weeks I found a measure of peace. And for a while there was genuine gladness I could serve my sick wife with the same grace and tenderness which I had felt from her during the days of my agnostic hardness.

But soon confusion set in again. Some friends redoubled their efforts at building our hope to the level of their faith. About two weeks after my conversation with Graham, I came to the point of rationalizing what the Lord had said about wanting to take Shirley to Himself. Perhaps what He really wanted was for me just to be willing to release her.

Shirley's parents and I wanted her to live as much as our faith healing friends did, so we considered a visit to Kathryn Kuhlman, but instead summoned a minister from out of state. She had a proven ministry of healing and we decided to trust her wisdom. After seeing Shirley alone, and praying with her, the woman announced that God had told her these facts: If I would demonstrate blind faith in the Bible's promises to heal, and take Shirley off her medicines and home from the hospital, she would improve daily and be healed quickly.

I felt impaled on the horns of an intolerable dilemma. If there was even a remote chance that Shirley's healing depended on removing her from the hospital, how could I ever live with myself if we didn't obey? But she was so helplessly sick and in constant need of pain killers. Her blood count had reached an all-time low and because her veins were collapsed the doctors had inserted a permanent tube into her leg, which meant confinement to a bed.

Against strong protests from the doctors we took Shirley home to her parents' house. Day by day her

197

condition worsened, though we had been told it would improve. Deprived of proper care she rapidly lost ground and her suffering increased. On the fourth frantic day I received a phone call from Graham. He and a friend wanted to come by the house for a visit.

When they arrived that evening his friend visited with Shirley's parents in the kitchen while Graham talked with us in Shirley's bedroom. He was quiet but insistent.

"Shirley, has God Himself told you plainly that He's going to heal you?"

Shirley hesitated and we looked at each other. Then slowly she began shaking her head No.

"What about you, Bill?"

I held back tears and reached across the bed for Shirley's hand. She was in such pain. Wearily I answered, "I guess not."

"What has the Lord said to you, Shirley?"

She hesitated again, then looking at me said in quiet confidence, "That He loves me—that He died for my sin—that He's merciful—that I can trust Him."

Graham smiled kindly. "That's wonderful. It doesn't mean that He won't heal you, Shirley, but as far as I can see it's not your testimony that He said He would. Others seem to think they hear that—and that's fine for them—but your faith has to rest on what the Lord's said to you, not on what He's said to someone else.

"Bill, if you knew that God intended simply to be merciful and loving, if there was even a chance He wasn't going to heal Shirley of leukemia, would you be doing anything different than you are now?"

My answer came without hesitation. "Yes, I'd have her back in the hospital where she could be comfortable." . . .

The hospital officials graciously readmitted Shirley the next day but the advance of her disease was irreversible. We were all helpless, and the swarm of her many counselors thinned to an infrequent straggler. Now there were round-the-clock tender ministrations from our families and from the nursing staff; and there were quiet night-time hours of silent sharing between Shirley and me—often spent to the rhythm of her fitful slumbers when in the darkness of a semiprivate hospital room we knew a communion of our love as deep as any that had ever gone before.

She had been readmitted on a Friday. The weekend was a parade of hospital routine, blood transfusions and new experimental drugs: though the progress of Shirley's pain and weakness had settled into a plateau, there were no signs of improvement. . . .

Wednesday at noon I called Graham to say that Shirley was in and out of a coma, her consciousness was more and more scattered, and things looked bad. He told me of a chapel in an Episcopal hospital across the street and suggested I spend time there in prayer. Before leaving I stood at the foot of Shirley's bed at a moment when she was coming around; when her eyes opened I was at the focus of her confused vision. She sat up, extended her arm toward me and called my name. After I smiled and touched her, she settled back into a quiet sleep and I left for the chapel.

Now Shirley sleeps the quiet sleep of those who rest in Jesus. He took her while I was praying in a lonely chapel. The page system had announced my name in the distance and I was warned of something. The rest was told by the strong arms and unashamed tears of my father, whom I met coming across the street to get me.

Having steeled myself against that moment, to begin with I walked numbly among the many things the bereaved accomplish in a merciful state of shock. Sometime during the afternoon I called Graham. He asked to see me as soon as things settled down and late that evening we met in his office. In the fold of his arms everything of my grief that was angry and frustrated and hurt was touched by his prayer and saw beginning hope of release. I wept the bitterest of tears and mourned the loss of the only person I had ever opened my soul to.

God glorified Himself in the death of Shirley DeSoto Farra on May 25, 1966, three weeks before I moved into the rectory of Church of the Redeemer and became a member of a growing charismatic community there. In Graham's household the hideous pain of separation from my wife of four months began slowly to be succored. It was not easy at times.

There were moments when I felt I had been duped by God. He enticed me from my agnosticism into the warmth and freedom of an exquisite relationship with one of His loveliest lambs. Then he withdrew her from my life leaving a naked relationship with Him. But it was not disembodied, I was to learn. I found the Jesus of my wife's soul embodied in a community of His servants gathered at Redeemer Church, and I joined Him there.

Appendix II
Pastoral Questions on Anointing for Roman Catholics

Sacraments and Blessings

Since writing the section on "Anointing the Sick" in *Healing*[1] I have learned several things I would like to share in relation to Anointing (the Sacrament of the Sick) and anointing.

FOR PHYSICAL HEALING TO REALLY OCCUR

First, I think it is really important that we do two things when we minister the Sacrament of the Sick:

1) that we do more to *build up the faith* of the people, and our own, and

2) that we spend *time* with our prayer.

As regards faith, I find that for Catholics belief in healing is still weak, in spite of the fact that the Church now emphasizes healing as the basic purpose of the sacrament of Anointing   healing on some level: spiritual, emotional or physical. Yet, it is as if priests and people still believe only in spiritual healing and are skeptical about physical healing.

Without identifying the sources, let me just share with you the kind of thing we can still read. Both of these quotations are from fine articles on the beauties of communal Anointing services:

---

[1] P. 276 ff.

No miraculous cures happened at the prayer service for the sick. Shared compassion. The experience of God being close. That's better than a cure.[2]

No physical miracles were performed that Sunday afternoon, but the healing power of the Lord through the Sacrament touched and healed them in many ways emotionally and spiritually. The people themselves said it was a beautiful experience and they felt the healing and renewing strength of the Lord come alive in them.

Both of these articles assume that it is normal for spiritual blessings to occur, but not for physical healing to take place. I can't help but compare this with a letter of advertisement that I received from Oral Roberts, offering to anyone who writes him, a little alabaster jar of oil. In his letter Mr. Roberts writes:

I have taken your vial oil to the Prayer Tower and prayed over it. It is going to be a powerful point of contact for divine healings for you. There is enough oil for you to use every day or as often as needed. I promise you it will be a faith releaser for the everyday divine healings you need— for yourself, for your loved ones, for forgiveness of sins, for every need you have, for every problem you face.

I doubt whether Oral Roberts asks himself whether or not this oil is a sacrament, but we cannot help but notice the paradox: he (1) seems to expect more to happen than most sacramental Christians *expect to happen* through the sacraments and (2) he encourages people to use it in their *daily* life when they are faced with sickness and other

---

[2] At this service 295 people were anointed. Nobody will quarrel with the fact that it's better to experience the closeness of God than a cure. But why set up the opposition, as if a person had to make a choice. Besides, the *purpose* of the sacrament is that a cure take place (perhaps just spiritually) and it is often *through* a physical cure that people experience the closeness of God. (In my experience, if our team had a chance to pray individually with 295 people for physical healing, we would expect that more than half would be improved or healed completely.)

needs. In a way, he is doing what we did in the early Church when the bishop blessed oil and the people took it home for use whenever they needed to pray for the sick. St. Genevieve (who died around 500 A.D.), for instance, used to anoint the sick for whom she cared and one day was distressed to find she had run out of oil and there was no bishop within reach it bless it.[3]

At the very least, in upholding the value of the sacraments, we need more faith in what Anointing can do. Does it make sense for Catholics to boast that they have the sacraments when, in reality, they, at times, seem to believe less in what Anointing can effect than some Protestants who simply use oil and believe that this anointing will accomplish wonders? As the official Rite for Anointing states:

> The anointing of the sick, which includes the prayer of faith (see James 5:14-16) is a sacrament of faith. This faith is important for the minister and particularly for the one who receives it. The sick man will be saved by his faith. ...[4]

We are encouraged to build up the faith of the people in what Anointing can do—its purpose: healing on every level of the sick person's being, sometimes spiritual, sometimes emotional, sometimes physical, but healing at some level.

As regards the second point, spending more time in praying with the sick, I think that many of the problems I described in the chapters on praying for large groups of people are also operative on a communal, or even an individual, Anointing. I think it would help if the priest can pray an individual prayer for the particular sickness after ministering the entire rite or after saying the words prescribed for Anointing:

---

[3] "Anointing of the Sick, 1 (Theology of)" by J. P. McClain. *New Catholic Encyclopedia* (New York; McGraw-Hill, 1967), Vol. 1, p. 570.
[4] *The Roman Ritual: Rite of Anointing and Pastoral Care of the Sick*, Introduction (Collegeville; Liturgical Press, 1974). p. 11.

Through this holy anointing
may the Lord in his love and mercy help you
with the grace of the Holy Spirit.
Amen.
May the Lord who frees you from sin
save you and raise you up.[5]

After the sacrament has been ministered, the priest or friends of the sick person can continue awhile in prayer, saying a prayer that is specific for the person's illness, and soaking the person in prayer if that seems indicated. Several times people have told me of healings they received during the sacrament of Anointing, which they did not receive during previous prayers for healing, so we should recognize that there is a real power operative in the sacrament.

NONSACRAMENTAL ANOINTING

Many Catholic priests are not aware of this but there is a blessing for oil which is nonsacramental—for oil which is blessed for everyday healing use, and which the people can then take home and use in praying for each other.[6]

This blessing for oil is contained in the old *Roman Ritual* (still in effect at the time of this writing) under the title "Blessing of Things for Ordinary Use," immediately after the blessing of lard and immediately before the blessing of oats. There is no indication that the *use* of this oil is limited to the sacrament of Anointing or to the

---

[5] *Op. cit.*, p. 52. Note that this prayer for anointing is a change from the earlier form of the prayer as contained in *Study Test II: Anointing and Pastoral Care of the Sick*, published by the Bishops' Committee on the Liturgy (Washington, D.C.; U.S. Catholic Conference, 1973), p. 9. That prayer (quoted in *Healing*, p. 276) reads as follows:

"May the Lord who freed you from sin heal you and extend his saving grace to you."

[6] For the material on this subject I am indebted to Father John Bertolucci, formerly vice-chancellor of Albany and now pastor in Little Falls, New York, and Father Eugene Selzer, special consultant for the St. Louis Archdiocesan Commission for Sacred Liturgy, Music and Art

bishop or priest (although its blessing is reserved to the bishop or priest).

Following is the text of the blessing:

BLESSING OF OIL

Priest: Our help is in the name of the Lord.
All: Who made heaven and earth.

EXORCISM

God's creature, oil, I cast out the demon from you by God the Father ✠ almighty, who made heaven and earth and sea, and all that they contain. Let the adversary's power, the devil's legions, and all Satan's attacks and machinations be dispelled and driven afar from this creature, oil. Let it bring health in body and mind to all who use it, in the name of God ✠ the Father almighty, and of our Lord Jesus ✠ Christ, His Son, and of the Holy ✠ Spirit, the advocate, as well as in the love of the same Jesus Christ our Lord, who is coming to judge both the living and the dead and the world by fire.

All: Amen.
Priest: Lord, heed my prayer.
All: And let my cry be heard by you.
Priest: The Lord be with you.
All: May He also be with you.

Let us pray.

Lord God almighty, before whom the hosts of angels stand in awe, and whose heavenly service we acknowledge; may it please you to regard favorably and to bless ✠ and hallow ✠ this creature, oil, which by your power has been pressed from the juice of olives. You have ordained it for anointing the sick, so that, when they are made well, they may give thanks to you, the living and true God. Grant, we pray, that those who will use this oil, which we are blessing in your name, may be delivered from all suffering, all infirmity, and all wiles of the enemy. Let it be a means of averting any kind of adversity from

205

man, made in your image and redeemed by the precious blood of your Son, so that he may never again suffer the sting of the ancient serpent; through Christ our Lord.

All: Amen.

(It is sprinkled with holy water.)[7]

Just as holy water, which is intended for everyday use, is to remind us of the water of Baptism, so also this oil, a sacramental, is to remind us of the sacrament of Anointing. Notice that the prayer speaks of "those who will use this oil" and assumes that they will be someone other than the priest who blesses the oil. In short, Catholics could well recover part of their heritage of praying for the sick by rediscovering some of the means which are already at hand—means similar to those which Oral Roberts and other evangelists have discovered for themselves through their study of St. James' epistle and other texts referring to healing. All we need is instruction in this matter: that priests learn about this prayer in the *Ritual*, which they are expected to use, and then proceed to instruct laypeople in how to use the oil and how to pray for members of their families in simple ways.[8]

OTHER REDISCOVERED BLESSINGS

In the same *Roman Ritual* there are a number of blessings special to various religious orders in which objects are blessed for healing purposes, much as in Acts we read about how handkerchiefs and aprons that Paul had used were taken to the sick and that their diseases

[7] *The Roman Ritual*, transl. by Philip Weller (Milwaukee; Bruce, 1964), p. 573.
[8] It is interesting to note that the letter sent out by Oral Roberts (and mentioned earlier) has a picture of Oral anointing his wife, and vice versa, and gives the prayer he uses. "Evelyn. I anoint you with oil in the name of Jesus, for God's great gladness of heart and for you to have many divine healings."

were cured and they were freed of demonic oppression (Acts 19:12). There are, for instance,

- —a blessing of St. Benedict's medal "for health of mind and body," special to Benedictines;
- —a blessing of oil for healing in honor of St. Serapion, special to the Mercedarian Order;
- —a blessing of water for healing, in honor of St. Raymund Nonnatus, special likewise to the Mercedarians;
- —a blessing of water for healing, in honor of St. Vincent de Paul, special to the Vincentians; and
- —a blessing of water for healing of every sickness of body and spirit, in honor of St. Peter Martyr, special to the Dominicans.

To give you an idea of the kind of blessing which has largely fallen into disuse, I here translate from the Latin, a blessing special to my own Dominican Order, for water in honor of St. Vincent Ferrer (our most renowned preacher who lived in the 14th century). This blessing is written in the lengthy style of medieval Latin, but notice the powerful faith for healing assumed in this prayer.[9]

BLESSING OF WATER FOR THE SICK, IN HONOR OF ST. VINCENT FERRER

Verse. Our help is in the name of the Lord.
Response. Who made heaven and earth.
Verse. May the name of the Lord be blessed.
Response. Now and forever.
Verse. O Lord, hear my prayer.
Response. And let my cry come to you.
Verse. The Lord be with you.
Response. And with your spirit.

---

[9] For Protestant readers: I recognize that there are difficulties you may have with certain aspects of this blessing (e.g., the invocation of a saint; although Catholics see this as being similar to the handkerchiefs touched to Paul—not deifying him, but using him as a point of contact with God). All I want to do is point out the powerful faith for Christ's healing in the history of Christianity which we need to recapture.

Let us pray.

Lord we humbly beg your majesty that you, who blessed the rock in the desert, so that when Moses struck it twice with his rod, water flowed forth in abundance (since by that act you wished to symbolize the sacrament of the Passion in the two beams of the Cross, represented by the double blow of the rod), through your kindness and clemency, working through the mystery of that same Holy Cross, sanctify this water by your great blessing, so that every sick person who drinks it, or who is sprinkled with it, will immeidately experience the health-giving effect of your blessing. Through Christ our Lord.

R. Amen.

I bless this water in the name of God ✠ the Father omnipotent, who created this element for its blessed human use, that it may serve to cleanse filth from body and soul, as elevated to this purpose by your wondrous omnipotence; that it may be a drink for those who thirst, a refreshment for those who languish, a way and a path for those who travel by sea; and may God who, by submerging the whole world in and through water, established a symbol beforehand of Baptism, the sacrament of the New Law, when he saved eight persons in the ark floating in the water, and who caused rain to fall on the earth 40 days and 40 nights when the cataracts of the skies were opened—may he bless ✠ this water and sanctify ✠ it, that it may heal the sick at the invocation of his name—and that of St. Vincent; that it may strengthen the weak, lift up the dejected, cleanse the impure, and restore health in a powerful way to anyone who asks. In the name of the Father , and of the Son and of the Holy Spirit.

R. Amen.

(The priest touches the bottle of water with the relic or image of St. Vincent and says:)

Let us pray.

Answer, Lord, our requests and, by the merits of St. Vincent, pour out the power of your repeated blessings upon this element of water which is touched by this relic, so that it may be a draught of health for the one who drinks it.

R. Amen.

In the name of the Father, and of the Son,　　and of the Holy Spirit.

R. Amen.

(The sign of the Cross should be made with the relic or image. Then the priest says:)

In the evening of life may St. Vincent help make our journey to Christ a safe one.

V. Pray for us, St. Vincent.

R. That we may be made worthy of the promises of Christ.

Let us pray.

O God, who brought a multitude of people to acknowledge your person through the wonderful preaching of your confessor,[10] St. Vincent—grant, we ask, that we may deserve to have as our reward in heaven the Judge whose coming he proclaimed upon this earth. Through Christ, Our Lord.

R. Amen.[11]

Notice also in this prayer that this blessed water is intended for drinking, and the healing is expected to come by God's using the normal use of water in an extraordi-

---

[10] Confessor in this sense means a witness to Christ, one who confesses his name.
[11] *Rituale Romanum* (New York; Benziger, 1953), pp. 483-484. The translation from Latin is mine.

nary way. In a smiliar way I believe we can pray a blessing for medicine, for orange juice, and for all fluids we may drink when we are sick, that God may reinforce and magnify the healing effects of these elements we naturally use in helping the healing process of the body.

A TESTIMONY TO
NONSACRAMENTAL ANOINTING

The following description comes from a person who took part in one of our healing workshops. At the very last session we blessed oil with the blessing given above and asked the people to pray for one another; the following is one person's experience of what happened (August, 1976):

... My purpose in attending the workshop was to learn more about the healing ministry, since I have been involved for about a year in visiting and praying with hospital patients. (The Clinical, Pastoral Education course I had taken was most helpful but was almost devoid of the spiritual dimension. I could never make the latter statement about last week!)

I would like to share with you something which this former skeptic experienced during the anointing on Friday, following the beautiful celebration of the Eucharist in the woods. Earlier that afternoon I had prayed for about an hour with two friends whom I met at the retreat. During their prayer they received a word of knowledge that I would receive some sort of special anointing. I was still skeptical. I have seen people in the hospital healed following prayer, but I really doubted that the power of the Lord could be given to *me*. I saw it only for others.

Anyway, as background: when I was 27 I gave birth to a full-term but unexpectedly stillborn daughter. As I fought my way out of the anesthesia (my other four children were delivered by natural childbirth with no medication), I was filled with fear and asked the doctor, "Is the baby all right?" "No, Barbara, it is not," he replied.

I should also mention that my own birth was a very

difficult forceps delivery in which my mother was in active labor for 25 hours due to the fact that her pelvic region was deformed early in her life by polio. (She had also been the driver in a serious automobile accident in which she was badly injured one month before my birth.)

At the anointing on Friday our prayer group of three was joined by three others. One of the two who had prayed with me earlier anointed me. As she began with my forehead I felt a powerful sensation of being placed under anesthesia. I felt the same ringing sensation in my ears that I have experienced when actually in the delivery room. I felt no fear, but only wonder, as I was drawn deeply into this experience. The others in the group around me became delivery-room personnel, nurses, anesthetist, etc. I relived the birth of my daughter and, simultaneously, my own birth—I could see and feel both taking place.

In this re-creation of both births Jesus became the physician and it was of him that I asked the question, "Is the baby all right?" (It was during the interval between the question and his answer that I saw that somehow the two deliveries were occurring simultaneously.) Jesus' strong but gentle answer came, "Yes, Barbara, the baby is all right. She is alive and so are you—you are both living in me."

I was completely unaware of the rest of the anointing, which ended for the group before I returned mentally. It was like a beautiful dream to which one wants to return upon awakening. I have never felt such peace, such love, such joy and I thank and praise Jesus, the blessed physician, for it.

When I once more became aware of those around me it was to see Sister Nancy returning to anoint my pulse with oil and to ask that my heart would beat as one with the Sacred Heart of Jesus. Then Jesus concluded this marvelous afternoon by having me "rest in the Spirit" right there among the leaves and twigs. This was another experience this skeptic hadn't even witnessed (I had been too tired to stay for prayer on the evening when it happened to so many.) In the resting I was again completely at peace and saw and felt at first a great light and then a soft darkness. I had the sensation of being completely alone though people told me afterward that they remained beside me praying. As I rested, Jesus told me that I was alone with him and I was not to feel lonely. He appeared to me then, asking me to rest in him and to release to him all my worries and burdens and to relax totally, trusting him.

When it was time to leave and return to my home, my children and my parish, I could truly say when asked, "Are you driving?"—"No, I'm flying."

Novels of Enduring Romance and Inspiration by

GRACE LIVINGSTON HILL

☐	12928	**TOMORROW ABOUT THIS TIME**	$1.75
☐	11506	**THROUGH THESE FIRES**	$1.50
☐	12846	**BEAUTY FOR ASHES**	$1.75
☐	12847	**THE ENCHANTED BARN**	$1.75
☐	10947	**THE FINDING OF JASPER HOLT**	$1.50
☐	2916	**AMORELLE**	$1.50
☐	2985	**THE STREET OF THE CITY**	$1.50
☐	10766	**THE BELOVED STRANGER**	$1.50
☐	10792	**WHERE TWO WAYS MET**	$1.50
☐	10909	**DAPHNE DEANE**	$1.50
☐	11005	**STRANGER WITHIN THE GATES**	$1.50
☐	11020	**SPICE BOX**	$1.50
☐	11836	**JOB'S NIECE**	$1.75
☐	11329	**DAWN OF THE MORNING**	$1.50
☐	11167	**THE RED SIGNAL**	$1.50

Buy them at your local bookstore or use this handy coupon for ordering:

Heartwarming Books
of
Faith and Inspiration

☐ 11710 **THE GOSPEL ACCORDING TO PEANUTS** $1.50
Robert L. Short

☐ 2576 **HOW CAN I FIND YOU, GOD?** $1.75
Marjorie Holmes

☐ 10947 **THE FINDING OF JASPER HOLT** $1.50
Grace Livingston Hill

☐ 10176 **THE BIBLE AS HISTORY** Werner Keller $2.50

☐ 12218 **THE GREATEST MIRACLE IN THE WORLD** $1.95
Og Mandino

☐ 12009 **THE GREATEST SALESMAN IN THE WORLD** $1.95
Og Mandino

☐ 12330 **I'VE GOT TO TALK TO SOMEBODY, GOD** $1.95
Marjorie Holmes

☐ 12853 **THE GIFT OF INNER HEALING** $1.95
Ruth Carter Stapleton

☐ 12444 **BORN AGAIN** Charles Colson $2.50

☐ 11012 **FASCINATING WOMANHOOD** Helen Andelin $1.95

☐ 13077 **TWO FROM GALILEE** Marjorie Holmes $2.25

☐ 12717 **LIGHTHOUSE** Eugenia Price $1.95

☐ 12835 **NEW MOON RISING** Eugenia Price $1.95

☐ 13003 **THE LATE GREAT PLANET EARTH** $2.25
Hal Lindsey

☐ 11140 **REFLECTIONS ON LIFE AFTER LIFE** $1.95
Dr. Raymond Moody

Buy them at your local bookstore or use this handy coupon for ordering:

Bantam Books, Inc., Dept. HF, 414 East Golf Road, Des Plaines, Ill. 60016

Please send me the books I have checked above. I am enclosing $_____
(please add 75¢ to cover postage and handling). Send check or money order
—no cash or C.O.D.'s please.

Mr/Mrs/Miss _____

Address _____

City _____ State/Zip _____

HF—5/79

Please allow four weeks for delivery. This offer expires 11/79.

INSPIRATIONAL FAVORITES

EUGENIA PRICE
St. Simon's Trilogy

☐	12712	Beloved Invader	$1.95
☐	12835	New Moon Rising	$1.95
☐	12717	Lighthouse	$1.95
		and	
☐	6485	Don Juan McQueen	$1.75
☐	8878	Woman To Woman	$1.50

HAL LINDSEY

☐	11545	The Liberation of Planet Earth	$1.95
☐	11132	Satan Is Alive And Well On Planet Earth	$1.95
☐	11259	The Terminal Generation	$1.95
☐	10382	There's A New World Coming	$1.95

Buy them at your local bookstore or use this handy coupon for ordering:

Bantam Books, Inc., Dept. PL, 414 East Golf Road, Des Plaines, Ill. 60016

Please send me the books I have checked above. I am enclosing $_____ (please add 75¢ to cover postage and handling). Send check or money order —no cash or C.O.D.'s please.

Mr/Mrs/Miss_____

Address_____

City_____ State/Zip_____

PL—3/79

Please allow four weeks for delivery. This offer expires 9/79.

Bantam Book Catalog

Here's your up-to-the-minute listing of over 1,400 titles by your favorite authors.

This illustrated, large format catalog gives a description of each title. For your convenience, it is divided into categories in fiction and non-fiction—gothics, science fiction, westerns, mysteries, cookbooks, mysticism and occult, biographies, history, family living, health, psychology, art.

So don't delay—take advantage of this special opportunity to increase your reading pleasure.

Just send us your name and address and 50¢ (to help defray postage and handling costs).